# Anxiety, Panic Attacks and **Agoraphobia** Made Simple

(Formerly Freedom From Agoraphobia)

A Practical, Medication–Independent Program For Just About Everyone

MARK EISENSTADT, M.D.

**Anxiety, Panic Attacks and Agoraphobia Made Simple: A Practical, Medication-Independent Program For Just About Everyone**
© 2012 by Mark Eisenstadt, M.D.

Cover Photograph by:
Mark Newman
MN.Golden.Alaska@gmail.com

Anxiety Chart by:
Lorelei and Steven Goldberg

ISBN: 978-0-9741512-1-2

*With loving thanks to my wife, Karen Marie for her endless proofreading and for her support in bringing this work about.*

# CONTENTS

# DISCLAIMER

This book contains a program of instructions I have given certain patients in the past to help them achieve freedom from Anxiety, Panic and Agoraphobia. It is meant for people experiencing these to use in consultation with a therapist or physician. The program includes educational information, self-observation, and experiments involving others. At times, the book recommends sweeping changes in one's life and how to cope with external changes. No instruction is right for everybody all the time. The program must therefore be tailored to each individual and that individual's circumstances. An appropriately trained physician or other professional should work with you to do such tailoring. Thus, this book does NOT take the place of a trained therapist or physician.

By means of this book, the author is certainly NOT able to provide medical diagnosis or treatment of any individual whom he has never met. Thus, the author makes no guarantee as to the safety or effectiveness of anyone's use of this book. In order to avoid situations in which the book may be inappropriate, it should be used only in consultation with a professional health care provider.

The reader must therefore assume all liability and responsibility for any adverse effects that could arguably be related to the use of this book. **Persons who do not accept total responsibility for all consequences of using this book are advised not to make any use of it.**

In addition, it should be noted that factual information has been modified to protect the privacy of patients, family members or colleagues in real life. Any resemblance to anyone is purely coincidental. The patient examples in this book are fictionalized variations and composites that do not identify any real individual in order to preserve confidentiality.

# PREFACE

Prefaces are problems. You want to get to "the real stuff." But maybe there is something in that Preface you need to know. So as soon as you open the book there is a problem. Do you skip the Preface and go directly to what you want to read? Or, do you slog through, reading a bunch of stuff about what you are finally going to get to read after you finish that darn Preface?

Usually, I skip them. Unless they are so short that they are not going to hold me up for very long anyhow (which this one is). Here's another idea—a Preface that tells you that it's okay to skip it. That's also what this is.

Instead, at the end of the book is an "About Face." It turns around and gives you information *about* this book—the author's background in the subject, how the book came to be written, what's in it, for whom it is written and suggestions for how to use it.

If you are a Preface-reader and want to know these things before you start, that's where to find them. If you want to get to the real stuff and get there now, go right ahead. You won't lose anything by jumping right in. In fact, if you want to start with the guts of the whole subject, turn directly to Chapter 4 — The Key To Panic Disorder.

Feel free. This book is for your liberation. It belongs to you.

*Mark Eisenstadt, M.D.*
*January, 2012*

# CHAPTER ONE

---

## Introduction to Anxiety, Panic Disorder and Agoraphobia

## Or

## What are they and do you have them?

---

Anxiety, Panic Disorder and Agoraphobia are closely related conditions involving anxiety and panic attacks, and behaviors designed to avoid them. Panic Disorder is simply the condition of having panic attacks. You probably do not need a description of these, but for anyone who does, here goes: panic attacks are episodes of feeling extremely frightened together with having a number of physical symptoms related to fear—such as shortness of breath, rapid heart rate, feeling your heart pounding, butterflies in the stomach, sweating, feeling weak-kneed, tingling in hands and feet, dizziness, feeling that you are likely to faint or go crazy or die and feeling that you or your surroundings are not quite real. These are all symptoms of "anxiety" — a word that covers the whole range of severity from mild worry to the extreme of intensity which is called "panic." Happily, few people experience all of these each time they have a panic attack. (If just reading that list of symptoms caused you to feel some of them, take heart — you're reading the right book.)

Panic attacks generally last from 20 minutes to one hour. You often feel drained or empty after they are over. Some people even feel a sense of relief or that the pressure has been released.

Often, it seems that the panic attack came on for no reason. Such panic attacks are called "Spontaneous Panic Attacks." As you work with this book, however, you will find that they usually are not spontaneous. Instead, many people have learned how they "work themselves into a panic attack." A common way to bring on a panic attack is to fear that you are going to have one and then become more and more anxious at the thought. This kind of anxiety is called "Anticipatory Anxiety" because it is anxiety created by the anticipation of something awful happening (the panic attack).

If you have panic attacks at least once a week or have feared having another one for at least four weeks, you meet the diagnostic criteria in Psychiatry for Panic Disorder. (See DSM IV in the reading list at the end if you want the full, official definition of the condition.)

I do not need to tell you that panic attacks feel terrible. In fact, it may be that people try to avoid this experience more than any other physical and emotional state. So people are very motivated to find ways to not have them. For many, it seems that panic attacks are brought on by particular places. A person trying to avoid panic attacks will, of course, avoid those places. As more and more places are identified as causing panic attacks, the individual's world becomes more and more restricted. Thus, in some few, severe cases, people will not leave their homes or even their beds.

Having panic attacks and a group of places that one avoids is called "Agoraphobia." The "agora" was the marketplace in old Greece. Hence, the word literally means: "fear of the marketplace." Since so many agoraphobics have trouble at the supermarket, perhaps this is not such an outdated idea after all.

The agoraphobic often develops an area close to home in which she feels safe. Usually, she has also identified other "safe places." The home of her parents may be one even if it is farther away from her own home than she normally feels comfortable going. A therapist's office may become a safe place. Also, there are usually "safe people." These are people (frequently close friends and relatives) with whom the agoraphobic feels safe. Thus, with a safe person, she is able to go outside her usual radius from home or to other places she avoids when by herself. The agoraphobic often says that she feels safer when she is with the "safe person" because "there is someone there to help if I have a panic attack." On the other hand, she is usually aware, if asked, that the safe person really does not have any special way of helping in the event of a panic attack. Also, young children and even infants can be "safe people" because the agoraphobic feels that with them she can go places she would avoid if she were alone.

You can see how natural it is for a person who has panic attacks to develop an avoidance pattern. So most people who have Panic Disorder also have Agoraphobia. Because of this, the two terms are often used interchangeably in this book. However, to be precise about it, there are some individuals who have an avoidance pattern but no panic attacks and there are others who have panic attacks but no avoidance pattern. (This is beginning to sound like Lewis Carroll's Cheshire cat.) As a result, there is officially a diagnostic distinction between Panic Disorder With Agoraphobia, Panic Disorder Without

Agoraphobia and Agoraphobia Without A History Of Panic Disorder. In my experience, they usually go together, so I will assume that this is the case for you. From here on, therefore, I will speak as if you have both panic attacks and an avoidance pattern. Since panic is the extreme of anxiety, then by definition, if you have panic, you have anxiety.

Agoraphobia (officially, "Panic Disorder With Agoraphobia") usually crops up in the '20s. For reasons we will examine later, it gets better and worse as the months and years go by. This means that most people experience periods of having many panic attacks alternating with periods of having very few. Until you solve it by the use of this book or effective therapy or working out your own solution, it always seems to come back.

Many more women develop Agoraphobia than do men. This does not mean that women are worse off, however. It seems that men often solve the same problems that result in Agoraphobia by turning to alcohol. Clearly, this is not better. Since you are reading this book, you are more likely to be a woman. So I will usually refer to panic sufferers and agoraphobics as "she" rather than using the clumsy "she or he", "she/he" or "s/he." If you are a man, don't worry. This book applies to you just as much in every way. You have probably succeeded in avoiding the worse choice of becoming addicted to alcohol. Bravo! And reading something that speaks of agoraphobics as "she" may even help you overcome any lingering "macho" tendencies, if you have any.

Agoraphobics tend to be masters (mistresses?) at concealing the fact of their condition. The list of excuses they invent for not going somewhere can be truly impressive. I have known patients who have had Agoraphobia for many years but whose families where completely unaware of it.

Different studies have found the prevalence of Panic Disorder and Agoraphobia to be 1.6% to 2.2%. This means that about one out of every 50 people will have it sometime in her life. Estimates have gone as high as one out of every 20!

The prevalence of depression in persons with Agoraphobia or Panic Disorder is over 50%. This makes good sense for reasons you will understand in Chapter 6. Also, some people give themselves a double whammy by having Agoraphobia and drinking alcohol as well.

## Assignments

Reading a book is never going to cure your Agoraphobia. Change is. Change comes about by making what you have read into something that is your own. You have to put it into practice and test it out. You must make discoveries about yourself and the world. You need to treat yourself and others differently and have new experiences. In a word: you have to grow.

One of the nicer facts about life is that growing offers a way out of every problem. This means that every problem has a solution that results from our becoming more whole, more complete people. We must open our eyes and hearts and minds to more of what is true and really happening, both inside us and outside us. This sometimes makes us more loving or more forgiving. We may need to become more accepting of our own and others' frailties. We often discover more of who we are. Sometimes we find beauty where we only saw ugliness. Sometimes we learn to laugh at ourselves. And sometimes we learn to cry.

There are many ways of dealing with problems that do not involve growing. One can use a medication or other chemicals to try to get rid of the feelings. One can change one's environment rather than oneself. One can try to compensate with food or relationships or excitement. You know the alternatives. We've all tried lots of them.

For those who seek it, however, there is a treasure to be found in the wilderness of each problem. And the seeker finally emerges as a more complete person.

But to grow takes doing. So, after each chapter, you will find assignments that will take you through the wilderness. They are designed to make what you have read something that is your own—both in your mind and in your experience. The assignments often tell you to write things down. This is very important. If you just do an assignment in your mind, the thoughts will evaporate as soon as you have your next thoughts. You will find that if you write down the assignment, it has a much different effect. The assignments are often not easy. (What that is worthwhile ever is?) But they will lead you where you want to go. If you walk the path…

# Assignments for Chapter 1

## 1. See your doctor

There are two vital pieces of information you need from your Primary Care Physician before you go on.

First, you need to know that you do not have one of the numerous physical conditions that can have the same symptoms as anxiety or panic. It could be quite disastrous if you assumed you had Agoraphobia when you really had a medical condition needing treatment that you never got. These conditions include thyroid disorders, certain heart problems, hypoglycemia, adrenal disorders and a number of others. See your Family Practitioner and tell her all of your symptoms. Ask to be checked out for the possible presence of a physical cause of those symptoms. Tell her that you are undertaking Panic Disorder treatment and need to know that you are not working on the wrong problem.

Second, ask whether it is harmful for you to have panic attacks. Although panic attacks are scary and uncomfortable, for most people, the physical stress of panic attacks is well within the range of what our bodies can safely tolerate. This is not surprising. If our built-in reaction to the threat of danger was itself harmful to us, our species would not have lasted very long. (Who would be around today if early man had keeled over with a heart attack at the roar of a sabre-toothed tiger?) So for your general peace of mind as well as for reasons that will appear later, it is most important that you learn whether there is truly any cause for you to fear panic attacks.

## 2. Find a group

If you are not already in one, find yourself a Panic Disorder or Agoraphobia support group. Try it out. If it is not to your taste, try another. Before you go, ask whether the members are working at overcoming their Agoraphobia or whether they believe it is incurable. Of course, if they believe it is incurable (and some do), find another group. This is a program for overcoming Panic and Agoraphobia—not just learning to live with it.

If there are really no groups in your area, think about starting one. Two or three people to work through this book together can make it much easier. If you cannot find anyone else with whom to work this program, you certainly can do it by yourself. Many people have—and quite successfully. Others walking the path with you can make it a lot more fun, however.

### 3. Define your Panic Attacks

Write out a list of the symptoms you have during a panic attack. Write down how often panic attacks occur and how long they last.

### 4. Define your Avoidance Pattern

Write down where you are and are not able to go. Include anything you are unable to do. Put your list in order of easiest to hardest. (We'll need this again for Chapter 9).

### 5. Define the waxing and waning of your Panic Disorder

Write out (as best you can) when your panic attacks started, when in your life they lessened and when they got worse. Include when your current period of panic attacks began. (You will see why in The Key To Panic Disorder.)

# CHAPTER TWO

---

# The Biology of Panic

## Or

## What Goes On In Your Body

---

One aspect of us is that we are biological beings – simply, we have bodies. The physical responses to anxiety that we experience during panic attacks are based upon the biology of these bodies. Many of the responses are caused by the release of adrenalin. Releasing adrenalin is the way our minds tell our bodies that it is necessary to either run or fight. This is the so-called "fight or flight" response. In other words, when we are frightened by something, our bodies get ready to either run away or physically attack whatever scares us. How do we do this?

---

First of all, our bodies go into high gear. Adrenalin causes our hearts to pump fast so that there is plenty of oxygen to give our muscles the strength to move fast and our brains the ability to think fast. But that oxygen needs to go to the right places. So the adrenalin directs the oxygen-carrying blood where it is needed and away from where it is not. It is needed in the muscles of arms and legs and in the brain. It is not needed in the skin and the digestive organs. Adrenalin is designed to cause the blood vessels of skeletal muscles and brain to enlarge so there can be more blood flow in these parts of our bodies. Meanwhile, the blood vessels of skin and digestive organs constrict in order to shunt blood away from where it is not needed. This results in "going pale with fear" because the blood has moved away from the skin. It also causes various sensations in the digestive organs such as cramps or "butterflies in the stomach."

Naturally, the adrenalin causes our hearts to beat faster which we experience as pounding. It also causes expansion of the breathing tubes in our lungs so that we get more oxygen. This, together with more rapid breathing, is the hyperventilation you experience during panic attacks.

Hyperventilation has a number of effects of its own. Most of these result from lowering the amount of carbon dioxide in our bodies. Did you know that we need a certain amount of carbon dioxide in our bodies? We do. When we breathe, we not only take in oxygen but we breathe out carbon dioxide. When we breathe fast, we lose the amount of carbon dioxide needed to keep us feeling normal. Loss of carbon dioxide causes us to feel dizzy, disoriented and to develop tingling and cramps in our hands and feet. You may have thought that you needed more oxygen. Sometimes it feels like that. But no - you needed more carbon dioxide! Hence, breathing into a paper bag helps.

We do not need much blood flow to our salivary glands so these shut down resulting in our having dry mouths. Our pupils dilate so we can take in the largest visual fields possible. This would presumably enable us to protect ourselves from whatever is coming at us from any direction. When startled, we notice that our hair may stand on end. This is much like the hair standing up on the back of a dog when it is threatened.

All of these changes are the result of adrenalin.

There are medications that block the effects of adrenalin. These are called beta-blockers. Some of the more common beta-blockers are Propranolol (Inderal), Atenolol (Tenormin) and Metoprolol (Toprol). They are used to prevent the effects of adrenalin. As a result, they make people who are experiencing adrenalin effects much more comfortable. Of course, they do not take away the emotional fear or anxiety. But imagine how much better you would feel if your heart stopped pounding, the butterflies in your stomach flew away and you were not hyperventilating.

On the other hand, drugs that either cause the release of adrenalin or have the same effects as adrenalin make people who have Panic Disorder quite uncomfortable. These are called "Sympatho-mimetics" which simply means that they mimic the action of the sympathetic nervous system. (This is the part of the nervous system that reacts to adrenalin). These drugs include caffeine, ephedrine, pseudoephedrine, stimulants, epinephrine, norepinephrine and many others. They are found in cold medicines, in dental anesthetics and in alternative treatments (dietary supplements) to give you energy sold at health food stores.

**Big Tip:** It is important therefore that you avoid these drugs if you want to avoid getting adrenalin effects. For example, it is a good idea to tell your dentist that you have Panic Disorder and cannot take anesthetics that have epinephrine or norepinephrine in them. Do you have to remember these words? No. To help you with this, I have included a letter for you to give to your physicians explaining these issues (See the next chapter.)

So now you know a lot of what goes on in your body that creates the feelings you call a panic attack. Next, we will look at what kind of a body you have to work with in the first place.

## Assignments for Chapter Two

### 1. Getting to know yourself – Part 1

As will be mentioned over and over, agoraphobics and people who have panic learn to suppress themselves so much and so often that they frequently end up not knowing what they want or who they are. But there is a you inside you who wants to live her life. The problem is finding out who she is. That's what this next assignment is all about.

Keep a notebook with you at all times. As you go through your day, write down everything you would do if you had a magic wand. Everything you wish you could do, could be or could have that you do not. Every change you would make in other people, your circumstances, the world and your life. Try to make your list as complete as possible. Add to it each time something else occurs to you. <u>Ignore your judgments!</u> It couldn't matter less if you think that wanting to be able to eat endless ice cream without gaining weight means that you are a pig. Write it down anyway. Do this for as many days as it takes to pretty much run out of new ideas. You can always add to it later.

Next, as you go through your days, write down everything you would <u>not</u> change. Would you have the same husband (even though you know just what changes he should make to become a much better one)? Would you keep your appreciation of nature? Are you glad of certain experiences you have had in your life? Do you like the part of you that makes you cry at sappy movies? Are you pleased with the remodel job on your kitchen?

Again, continue with this until you run out of new entries to make.

Now what? Just put the notebook away where no one will find it. And start to notice how different you feel for having done this assignment.

## 2. Your Anxiety Diary

Whenever we want to change something, it must become a focus of our attention. In fact, it often must become the first and foremost focus of our attention. Have you ever undertaken a really significant change like stopping smoking or losing a lot of weight or becoming less critical? If so, you know that it doesn't work to make the decision to do it and then forget about it and just go on about your usual daily affairs. In no time flat, you'll be right back doing the same thing you always did. So if you are to succeed, making that change must become a priority – often, the first priority.

You have to pay a great deal of attention to what you are doing that you want to change. You must learn all about it: What causes you to do it? What stops you from doing it differently? When does it get triggered? What is the good you get out of it? Are there alternatives? Why aren't you doing them?

In other words, what you want to change will have to become something you are constantly aware of and constantly working on. People just don't make big changes by means of half-hearted efforts such as saying: "Oh, I'll pay attention to that when it comes up." If we are not continuously on guard against that urge to eat or smoke or snap at others, we'll be back doing it before we know what hit us.

Naturally, I wouldn't be going on about this if it did not apply to Panic and Agoraphobia. In just the same way as making these other changes, overcoming Panic and Agoraphobia must become your priority. You must learn everything you can about your anxiety so that it doesn't creep up and take over before you know what's happening. All experiences of anxiety and panic must now be made to serve your goal of freedom from them. You are now living in one of those situations where the only erroneous experiences are those you do not learn from. And this is why it is so important to keep an Anxiety Diary.

Here's what to do:

Get a notebook and begin to keep track of your levels of anxiety as you go through the day. Rate your anxiety on a scale of 0 to 10 where 0 means you are completely calm and 10 means the most severe panic you have ever had. Get a timer and set it to time 4-hour intervals. (There are quite inexpensive wristwatches that can do this.) Note down your anxiety levels at 8 A.M., Noon, 4 P.M., 8 P.M. and Midnight if you are up. <u>Do This Every Day!</u> Note also any events that caused the anxiety levels to be as they were. This is *entirely important* if you are serious about overcoming panic and Agoraphobia. Keep your Anxiety Diary going from now on. You will need it later. But doing it will also begin to affect your experience immediately.

Why? Because this is treating yourself lovingly. Yep, lovingly. By keeping your Anxiety Diary going, you are periodically throughout the day keeping an eye on yourself and asking yourself: "How am I doing?" and "Why is it going like that for me?"

Remember that old Gershwin song, "Someone To Watch Over Me"? Well, guess what? <u>You</u> are watching over you. And maybe no one has done this for a long time. A very long time. Especially the most important person – you!

# CHAPTER THREE

## The Physiology Of Panic And Agoraphobia

### Or

### What Kind Of Body You Have To Begin With

Although there are no physical differences in people who have Panic Attacks that explain the condition, there are some differences that certainly contribute to it. For example, there is evidence that people with Panic Disorder have an increased sensitivity to adrenalin. Genetic research is under way and it appears that there is a genetic propensity to having Panic Attacks. It is already well established that Panic Disorder and Agoraphobia are familial. This means that they occur much more frequently in members of the same family than in persons who have no relatives with these conditions. On the other hand, it certainly can occur in persons who have no such relatives. Also, it does not occur in everybody who <u>does</u> have relatives with the conditions. But there is a greater likelihood if there are other family members who have them. It appears that heredity results in biological differences that are part of the cause for some people.

When a group of people who have Panic Disorder is compared to a group of people who do not, various physical differences can be identified. Not everyone in the Panic Disorder group has those physical differences, but far more people in that group have the differences than do persons in the non-Panic Disorder group. Here are some of those differences:

A chemical called Lactate (or lactic acid) has been noted to frequently cause panic attacks in persons with Panic Disorder. Sodium Lactate is very commonly used as the basic solution in intravenous fluids given in hospitals. It is important to tell your doctor that you have Panic Disorder and cannot take it. (This is included in the letter for physicians at the end of the chapter.)

Mitral Valve Prolapse Syndrome (MVPS) is seen in more than 50 percent of people with Panic Disorder. This is a condition in which the leaflets of the mitral valve in the heart allow some blood to go backwards. This occurs in almost everyone to some extent. In most people with panic, MVPS (also called "Barlow's Syndrome") is a benign condition requiring no treatment. However, it may cause you to have various sensations that may be very uncomfortable when you do not know what is going on. Some people experience a "floppy" feeling in their chests. Others experience the sensation of their hearts beating in their throats. Many times people go to their doctors because of these feelings but are told that there is nothing wrong. If this happens to you, don't think you are imagining things. The condition is there and it is causing the feelings you are having. It is just that the feelings are not dangerous for you no matter how uncomfortable they may be and they do not need treatment. (That is what the doctor means by "nothing wrong.") The condition can be diagnosed by an echocardiogram. This is a painless test that will tell you exactly how your mitral valve is performing. If you or your doctor are concerned that you may be one of the rare individuals who has a case of MVPS requiring treatment, she can order an echocardiogram for you.

Here are some more anomalies (which means differences - not abnormalities) seen in people who have panic: First, there is a great sensitivity to hormone changes. Thus, hysterectomy,

PMS, thyroid hormone, and adrenal hormones such as cortisone can all make panic attacks more likely. Also, people who have panic are more sensitive to bright lights, especially the fluorescent lights found in large stores. This has been confirmed by using the electroencephalogram or "brain wave" test. A way to enhance the EEG is to do it after a person has been deprived of sleep. When especially sensitive electrodes (wires called "nasopharyngeal leads"), are placed in the noses of sleep-deprived individuals, clear differences between panic sufferers versus other people have been identified. More such differences will doubtless be discovered in the near future because of the new brain-imaging technologies that have been developed such as P.E.T and S.P.E.C.T. scans.

The list of physical differences goes on and on. It will certainly be added to as more research is done. (Lucky you - not really.) A few of the more important ones affecting how you feel are as follows:

Galvanic Skin Response or GSR measures skin resistance to a tiny electrical current. As people relax, the skin resistance goes down. In fact, just repeating the measurements shows a decrease as time goes by. Not so for panic sufferers. Perhaps this reflects the continued high startle response seen in people with panic even after repeated stimuli.

Panic Disorder patients have a much higher sensitivity to medications than other people. Thus, when medications are prescribed for the treatment of Panic Disorder, they need to be used in far smaller doses than when they are prescribed for people with other conditions (such as depression). I have frequently observed the development of many side effects in agoraphobics at normal doses of antidepressant medications. To be helpful, these must be started "lower and slower" than usual. Then, if need be, they can gradually be increased.

Lastly, it is clear that being simultaneously exposed to a number of confusing stimuli such as lights, sounds, conversations, heat and bodily sensations all together create disorientation and the release of adrenalin in people with panic far more easily than in other people. You can see why agoraphobics have trouble in such places as crowded grocery stores. And you can see that there is a physiological reason for why you may prefer to go after hours when the store is quiet and few people are there.

The various anomalies or physical differences lead to panic attacks in an indirect as well as a direct way. For example, people with panic not only have an adrenalin reaction to multiple stimuli all coming in at once, but there is a reaction to this reaction. You might wonder: "What's wrong with me that

I feel so weird in situations that pose no problem for other people? Am I crazy? Am I seriously ill and no one has found the problem? What if I have cancer and no one knows?" I'm sure you can see how this can work itself into a panic attack.

What's the answer? **Read this chapter!**

When you do, you will realize that there are many physical differences that you have. And the medical profession may not yet recognize many of them. So you are not crazy. There are real processes going on in your body causing many of your unusual sensations. But just because they are there does not mean that you are having symptoms of something serious. In fact, you are in the same boat as everyone else:

Current medicine is able to identify most serious illnesses. If it has not found one in you, you probably do not have one. Just like everybody else. If medicine has not found a serious illness in a non-agoraphobic, she probably does not have one. No guarantees, but she probably does not. And if medicine has not found a serious illness in you, you probably do not have one. In other words, your unusual physical sensations and reactions make you no more likely to have a serious illness than any non-agoraphobic who has likewise had nothing serious diagnosed.

Read that again. It will rid you of a number of panic attacks. Just bear it strongly in mind the next time you find yourself "what if-ing" about some strange sensation you are having. You can truthfully tell yourself: "Oh, yeah. Here it is – an unusual sensation and me worrying about what it means. But now I know that it is normal for people with panic to have strange sensations. And now I also know that I am no more likely to have anything seriously wrong with me than people who do not have these sensations. If I have had it checked out and my doctor found nothing serious, there is every chance that this is just one of those annoying Panic Disorder sensations."

## Conditions Causing Panic Attacks

As was discussed in the first assignment for Chapter 1, there are physical conditions that can cause the symptoms of a panic attack. Thyroid and adrenal hormones can be released in increased amounts as a result of various disorders of these glands. For instance, hyperthyroidism and hypothyroidism can both cause panic attacks. Also, adrenal disorders such as Cushing's disease can do this. Hypoglycemia is a non-hormone condition that gives people panic attacks. A Glucose Tolerance Test can diagnose it. In this test, you are given a drink of glucose (a sugar) after which your blood levels of glucose are measured at various times. If you are having this test, it is a good idea to keep notes as to what you felt at different times during the test. That way, you can correlate how you felt at different times with the blood glucose levels you had at those times. If your panic attacks resulted from low levels, then you would have correlated the symptoms with the particular blood levels that caused them.

## After a Panic Attack

The way most of us are built, our bodies cannot keep releasing and reacting to adrenalin for very long. Just as we become emotionally desensitized to emotional stimuli when they keep being repeated, we also become physically desensitized to repetitive physical stimuli. If the creature from the black lagoon were to stay on screen long enough for us to really examine it, it would stop being scary. Likewise, we might love cherries but, if we were to eat them day after day, our taste buds would get desensitized and the cherries wouldn't remain so enjoyable.

Our bodies react to adrenalin. But they can't keep reacting to it all that long. Usually, 20 to 30 minutes and the body stops reacting. An hour is the outside amount for most people. On the other hand, I have often heard from patients that they have had panic attacks that lasted all day. If they really pay attention, however, they find that their hearts did not keep pounding at a high rate all that time. And they certainly did not keep hyperventilating or they would have passed out and the body would have returned to its normal, resting state. Instead, if they time it, those "all-dayers" come to realize that their panic symptoms do not last very long. Their bodies take a break. After a while of recovery, they may have worked themselves into another panic attack, but again, the symptoms lasted a fairly short time. It just seems like hours and hours because it's so unpleasant at the time. If you keep track of how long panic symptoms are actually lasting, you are likely to be in for a pleasant surprise.

After a panic attack, it seems as though there is less anxiety and less adrenalin floating around than usual. People often describe a feeling of being drained and completely relaxed after a panic attack.

You know that hard rubber pressure release valve on the lid of your pressure cooker? The one that blows out if the pressure is allowed to get too high, putting spaghetti sauce all over the ceiling? Well, for many people, a panic attack is like that pressure valve blowing out: All the pressure is released and there is peace. (Usually, panic attacks do not mess up the ceiling.) I have known agoraphobics who have times of wishing they had a panic attack, just to kind of "get it all out already" and be able to really relax. So, for many people, after the storm of the panic attack is over, at least there is a kind of reward in the sense of rest that follows.

## Dealing With The Medical Profession

When I was treating Agoraphobia 40 years ago, most physicians did not have any idea what the condition was. The situation has improved greatly since then. Now, the average Family Practice physician will have heard of it and know some of the basics about its symptoms. That's the good news. The bad news is that unless she has had some special training or experience with Panic Disorder, your physician may be fairly uncertain about how to deal with you. Obviously, it is not calming to be in the hands of an anxious physician. Also, she needs to know some of the facts we just discussed about your physiology.

On the next page, I have written a summary of the things your physician needs to know about treating you. Depending upon your physician, it may or may not be difficult to get her to read it. Once she does, however, I'm willing to bet that she'll find it had some useful information for her.

I am putting it on a separate page so that you can make a copy of it to give to her. (Physicians are much more willing to read a sheet of paper than to be handed a book. You can trust me on this.) Keep a copy of it in your Emergency Kit (see Assignment #3)

# Information For Physicians Regarding Panic Disorder

Your patient is working through a program for overcoming Panic Disorder. As part of this, I have advised giving you this information.

Having Panic Disorder means that your patient may undergo a major autonomic discharge coupled with extreme fear at any time. Panic attacks are most likely to occur in situations that are difficult or embarrassing to leave at a moment's notice. **Your office is one such situation.** Your patient is much less likely to have a panic attack if she feels she can leave whenever she needs to. Your understanding of this fact will help greatly.

Panic symptoms include tachycardia, hypertension, extrasystoles, hyperventilation (experienced as shortness of breath), paresthesias, flushing, tremor, shaking, G.I. cramps, diarrhea, nausea, headache, vertigo and, rarely, syncope. They usually last for 5 to 20 minutes but can continue longer in some cases. Unfortunately, you may need to postpone your examination in order to obtain baseline data as opposed to panic-induced findings.

Sympathomimetics, stimulants and lactate usually trigger panic attacks and should be avoided. Disorders of the thyroid, adrenal and glucose metabolism can do likewise and should be ruled out. Mitral Valve Prolapse is a common associated finding.

Parenteral benzodiazepines (not oral) are one of the few effective treatments for a panic attack in progress. Unless there is some specific reason such as an unusually prolonged or severe episode, this treatment is generally not required.

Finally, the most important point is that your patient has experienced many panic attacks and is working through a program for dealing with them. Consequently, **your patient knows best what is needed.** Physicians are therefore well advised to give patients the lead if a panic attack occurs during an appointment.

Mark A. Eisenstadt, M.D

# Assignments for Chapter Three

## 1. Getting to know yourself – Part 2

Now that you've put your finger on what you would and wouldn't change, what else are you like? Are you smart, pretty, sloppy, caring, responsible (of course you are), cowardly, creative, moody, critical, sociable, funny, irritable, strong, guilty, sweet, or what?

Start a list (with examples) as they occur to you. Again, ignore judgments. (You can put down "judgmental" if you want. Then move on to the next characteristic.) There will be many opposites. Sometimes we are smart and sometimes dumb. Put them both down on your list with their examples.

Cheri Huber, a Zen teacher, has written some excellent material on this subject. She looks at people as having developed "sub-personalities" – sort of as though we are many different personalities inside. It can be very useful to identify these sub-personalities and be aware of when we are being one or another of them. (See recommended reading later on.)

## 2. Continue your Anxiety Diary

## 3. Your Emergency Kit

One of my favorite psychiatrist authors (D. W. Winnicott) dedicated one of his books: "To my patients who have paid to teach me." So true. I think a therapist has failed to attend the most important school there is if she ignores the many creative and effective solutions people have devised to deal with their own problems. Thus, it was my patients who taught me to advise agoraphobics to always leave themselves an exit from any situation they enter.

Another solution developed by my patients is the Emergency Kit – a collection of items to enable them to deal with whatever might befall when out in the world. You probably have one – even if it is only called your purse or briefcase. In this assignment, I am passing along some of the excellent ideas other people with panic have worked out in the creation of their Emergency Kits (and some of my own). If you do not have one, definitely put one together. If you already have yours, you may want to add to it from the list below:

- Cell phone or Emergency CB radio.

- Cab fare.

- Some Benzodiazepines.

- First aid basics (band aids, antiseptic, adhesive tape, gauze pads).

- Aspirin.

- Snake bite and/or bee sting kits.

- Flashlight.

- AAA card.

- "In Case of Anticipatory Anxiety" Instructions (Ch. 14).

- "In Case of Panic" Instructions (Ch. 14).

- "Information For Physicians Regarding Agoraphobia" (Ch. 3).

- Notebook including Anxiety Diary (Ch. 2).

- Pen.

- Swiss Army Knife.

- Pepper Spray (if legal)

- Matches or lighter.

- Hotel-type sewing kit.

- Kleenex.

- Hair Spray - One-ounce sprayer. (Yep – men, too. Can you guess why? See the end of Chapter 4.)

- Whistle or siren.

- Paper bag for breathing into.

- Motion sickness bag.

- Space blanket (looks like aluminum foil – sold in camping stores)

- Emergency food

# CHAPTER FOUR

## The Key to Panic Disorder

### Or

### The Secret of What's Behind It All

Here is the key that unlocks the door to life without Panic:

It is the word "traps."

We develop panic attacks when we're trapped in our lives. We stop having panic attacks when we escape from those traps. We go in and out of periods of having panic attacks as we go in and out of periods of being trapped in the our lives. It's that simple!

This is why people will have panic attacks for a number of years and then, apparently, get over them. To their great disappointment, the panic attacks come back after more years have passed, seemingly for no reason. But there _is_ a reason. If we look at what has been going on in the individual's life we find that she was in a trap when the panic attacks began, had gotten out of the trap which caused them to get better and somehow slid back into another trap resulting in their return.

But what _is_ a trap? A trap is any situation we do not want to be in but from which we can see no acceptable escape. Straightforward enough, right? Read on. You will see that this simple definition – again: *any situation we do not want to be in but from which we can see no acceptable escape* -- contains all sorts of clues to the solution to Panic Disorder and Agoraphobia.

Traps can be big or little. They can last for minutes or years. They can have obvious exits or they can be nigh on impossible to find a way out of. They can be completely internal to the person with panic or they can involve all sorts of external circumstances and people.

Let's look at some:

Here's a common one that can last for decades if not a person's entire life:

Sylvia is growing up with a father who sexually molests her and a mother who drinks and refuses to admit what is going on. Sylvia has a friend who had the same problem with her own father and who told her teacher about it. Her father was sent to jail. Now, the whole family blames Sylvia's friend for the fact that they have to be on Welfare. They do not have many of the things they could afford when Dad was there to bring home a paycheck. Sylvia certainly does not want to have everyone in <u>her</u> family angry with her. But on the other hand, the weekend is coming. And that's when Mom goes out drinking and Dad will be coming to Sylvia's bedroom. The result? Sylvia has a panic attack. (Not surprising, huh?)

At 17, Sylvia grabs the opportunity to get out of the trap at home by leaving high school to marry her steady boyfriend, Darrell. Sylvia's panic attacks go away and it looks like her problems are over. She becomes pregnant and has a beautiful daughter whose smile is the light of her life.

But Darrell's company goes broke and he loses his job. As months go by and Darrell is unable to find another job, he becomes increasingly short-tempered. He begins to stay out evenings and comes home smelling of alcohol. When Sylvia comments that their limited money might be better spent paying the bills, Darrell flies into a rage and hits her. Soon, the drinking, arguments and physical abuse have become commonplace in Sylvia's life. And she can see no way out.

Darrell has told her that if she leaves he will find her and kill her. (He demonstrated what he meant by a slap in the face.) In any case, Sylvia can see no way to support herself and her baby. She does not even have a high school diploma with which to find a job.

One evening, she sits in her bedroom waiting for Darrell to come home from the bar and knowing that an argument and a beating are coming with him. In her mind, she struggles to find a solution but keeps running into the same barriers as always. Darrell can't find a job. The economy is bad. He has no training for skilled work. He won't stop drinking. There is no way to avoid a fight when he comes home. Even if she does not say anything to him, he'll just get mad at that. If only she could run away. But where would she go? And she has no money. And Darrell said he'd kill her. And the baby needs things... And...and...

She sits there in despair, waiting for the sound of the car in the driveway.

The next day, Sylvia and her black eye are in the supermarket. She is stuck in a long line at the checkout counter. The baby is getting tired and irritable. It's hot and the fluorescent lights are bothering her. But she can't leave. She needs the diapers, formula and other items in the shopping cart. She desperately thinks: "Why don't they call for another cashier?" There is only the one checkout line and the cashier in that one is obviously a friend of the old lady she is waiting on. The two of them are chatting away, oblivious to the long line in which Sylvia is stuck. The cashier keeps talking and interrupting the old lady from writing a check for her purchases. The line isn't moving. There is no way out. The heat and light make Sylvia dizzy. She is sweating. Her heart begins to pound. Suddenly, Sylvia finds that she is having a full-blown panic attack. It's the first since she left home almost two years ago.

Naturally, Sylvia can now easily develop an avoidance pattern that includes going to the supermarket. The next time she thinks of going there, she will remember this panic attack and begin to feel anxious at the thought of going back. If she goes anyway, she may well have another panic attack. Especially if she gets caught in another long checkout line. She may believe that the panic attacks are the result of being stuck in the supermarket situation. In a small way, she would be right. But in a larger way, Sylvia will have panic attacks one place or another. She'll even have them at home until she gets out of the trap she is in with Darrell. If that trap goes on for years or even decades, her panic attacks will go on for years or even decades.

Often, the panic attacks themselves serve to indirectly improve the trapped situation. For example, Sylvia might go to a doctor or counselor who might help her to find ways out of her abusive marriage. Or Darrell might actually feel a bit better about himself now that his wife needs him to help her go to such places as the supermarket. So the return of Sylvia's panic attacks might make the marriage somewhat less unpleasant for both of them. But even if this happens, as long as Sylvia is in the trap, she will have panic attacks. And when she gets free of the trap, she will be free of them. (We will see how Sylvia does this and her panic attacks stop in Chapter 12.)

Let's look at some other traps:

The Little League Mom typifies another kind of situation I have often seen. She lived in a beautiful home in a beautiful town, had a caring husband and an athletic 14 year old son. Her son was a star on the local Little League team and the team had been the state champions more than once. (This probably looks pretty good until you learn that for her, it meant not having a life.)

The entire family was centered on the celebrated son's Little League activities. And Mom was the one who had to make it all happen. The family traveled to all the Little League games - which were often held in other states or in Canada. Mom had to do all the packing for everyone including Dad because he couldn't be counted on to even bring matching socks. (Would it surprise you to hear that she often described Dad as: "just like having another kid"? I'll bet it wouldn't.)

She would lay out everyone's clothes for the trip, pack all the food, get the maps, arrange for the mail, call the police to keep an eye on the house while they were away and so on. The Little League moms cooked for the team and for the dads. She also had to drive her son to and from practice every day, attend meetings of Little League parents, do fund-raising for team uniforms and supplies, and on and on. The bottom line? Almost all of her time was devoted to Little League activities. She was ready to scream.

Why not quit? Well, was she going to stand up in front of her friends and be the only mom who did not care enough about her son to support his great effort and success in athletics? Certainly not!

The result once again was practically a foregone conclusion -- panic attacks. (We'll also see how she solved her problem later on.)

Another person with an obvious trap was Audrey who had recently put her mother in a long-term rehab hospital because of a broken hip. She had done so with the greatest reluctance and only after exhausting all other possibilities. The reluctance was because Audrey had heard all sorts of horror stories about rehab hospitals: People were neglected there. They were given the wrong medications. No one came when the patient called. Sometimes patients were abused or left to lie in their own waste for hours or even days before anyone took notice. Audrey knew that sometimes older people die after breaking a hip. And so forth.

Nonetheless, her mother's physical needs were way beyond what Audrey could manage at home. And there was no one else to provide the care. Finally bowing to the inevitable, Audrey had her mother admitted. Her fear was so great, however, that Audrey spent all day every day at her mother's side -- making sure that none of the disasters occurred. Audrey's husband and children were left to fend for themselves. They did not accept this easily. The staff of the hospital also complained that Audrey was driving them crazy (which she was). They constantly pressed for her to go home. But Audrey could hardly compound the sin of having put her mother in such a place by leaving her to the harm that would surely befall if no one were there to prevent it.

Result? You got it – panic attacks. (More about Audrey later.)

Lastly, let's look at a very temporary trap - the so-called "bad drug trip." Here's how this goes:

Cody and his friends decide to "drop some acid" (take LSD). Half an hour after taking it, Cody is happily enjoying the various bizarre colors, shapes and other hallucinations he is having. At one point, the thought comes: "Wouldn't it be great if this went on forever?" This is followed by another thought: "How do you know it won't?" Cody has heard stories of people whose LSD use resulted in their having hallucinations permanently. To reassure himself, Cody concentrates on a picture across the room, trying to get it to appear as normal. But it still seems to be glowing and pulsing – alternately getting larger and smaller. Then, it assumes some strange shapes – no longer being a rectangle.

This increases Cody's worries that his hallucinations will never go away. He tries harder to get rid of them but they remain despite all his efforts. He feels he must stop being on his "acid trip" in order to reassure himself that he can control it. But there is no way to stop. He becomes frightened. His fear then appears as dancing lights and animal shapes coming towards him. Cody panics. His heart is racing and feels as though it will burst out of his chest. He seems to not be able to get enough air – the room is too small and all the air is almost used up. He must run outside before he suffocates. But his knees feel weak and unable to support him. He must get out but he can't but he must but he can't...

Indeed, most "bad trips" due to hallucinogens are actually panic attacks. These panic attacks are all the result of the very same trap -- people becoming convinced that they need to stop experiencing the effects of the drug when they have no choice but to go on experiencing those effects for the next several hours until the drug wears off. Usually, this is triggered by some unwanted experience such as unpleasant hallucinations, feeling out of control or fearing "going crazy." As a result, the drug-intoxicated state that had originally seemed desirable becomes intensely undesirable.

And this brings us back around to our original definition of a trap: an unwanted situation from which we can see no acceptable way out. If the situation had not become unwanted, Cody would have happily experienced the drug effects and no panic attack would have occurred. Indeed, "talking people down" from bad drug trips (so common in the 70's and 80's) consisted of persuading them to not resist the drug effects. They were instead encouraged to simply allow the experience to run its course. Thus, the trap would cease to be one because they had changed the first half of the equation -- the desire to get out.

One of my early patients went through several steps in learning about traps in therapy. At first, she learned what her major trap was. (Let's call it her "Life Trap" since it is the trap her life was in overall.) With much difficulty, she worked her way out of it. After that she would come in having sometimes had a good week and sometimes a bad one. Since we knew that there was no longer a major Life Trap going on, the recurrence of panic attacks had to mean that she had gotten into some small "Day-to-Day Trap."

"How have you gotten trapped this week?" I would ask. "I haven't," she used to say at first. "The panic attacks just came out of the blue."

This would leave no choice but the tedious process of going over the whole week day by day. What had she done Monday? Had she wanted to do what she did? Had she made plans that she was really comfortable with? Had she allowed herself to be pushed into a commitment to do something or go somewhere that she really wished she could get out of? Had she had strong feelings about something? Feelings that she felt she could not or should not feel and express? What about Tuesday? No? No traps? What about Wednesday?...

Sooner or later, we would discover what it was. Then, we would find a way out of the trap and the panic attacks would stop. And the next time she came in having had a bad week, we would go through the process all over again. But each time, she learned more about what traps were and how she got stuck in them. And she learned what being true to herself really was.

It did not take very long before she would come in having had a bad week and I could simply ask: "So how did you get trapped?" She now knew enough to be able to look over her week by herself and figure out what the trap had been and how to better handle the situation. This was close to the endpoint of our treatment. After that, when she had panic attacks, she asked it herself: "How have I gotten myself trapped?" And she could figure it out for herself. She took the final step when she developed the ability to "see a trap coming" - she would not allow herself to be put in a situation that she knew would be a trap for her.

Then what? Success!! No more panic attacks!

More to come about how to get out of traps when we talk about therapy in Chapter 12.

# Assignments for Chapter 4

## 1. Identify your traps

If you have trouble, there is a lot about how to do this in Chapter 11. However, it is a good idea to make a start on it now.

Write down all traps that came to your mind as you read this chapter. Do you already know what your current overall "Life Trap" is? If so, write it down together with all the reasons you want to get out but cannot.

Have you had some little Day-to-Day Traps during the past week? (Like feeling you must go somewhere but being unable to?) If you have, write down every one you can recall. Start a running diary called "Traps" in a notebook. Each time you find yourself in one, write down the date and what the trap is. You don't have to find a solution to it. For now, it is enough to simply identify and record it.

## 2. Review your panic history

Look over your response to the Chapter 1 assignment of writing down the periods in your life when you had more (and fewer) panic attacks. See if you can identify the traps that caused each period of increased panic attacks. Write down your results.

## 3. Field Trips

Field Trips are an essential part of this program. If you skip doing them, you may as well put this book down now. It will not work for you. Simple as that. Field Trips are experiments in treating the world around you differently and checking out whether your assumptions about how the world will respond are really true. In this chapter, we have been getting down to the nitty gritty of why life has been as it has. This is also a good time to begin giving yourself experiences in living differently in the world. Read the "Experiments" section of Chapter 14. From here on, devise and take field trips at least weekly. To start with, simply get out and go somewhere for at least a half hour a day. It doesn't have to be difficult for you although it is preferable if it is somewhere you don't normally go. Make your field trips fun as often as possible. Fun is fine. Take others along if you like. That's great. But get out and do them!

## 4. Anxiety Diary

Continue your Anxiety Diary – especially during Field Trips.

## Hair Spray?

Last and certainly least, the purpose of the hair spray in the Emergency Kit is in case you get something that stains – like ink - on your clothes. Quickly apply the hair spray. It stops the stain from setting and you can wash the stuff out when you get home. (An agoraphobic beautician told me about this -- truth.)

# CHAPTER FIVE

## The Psychology Of Panic Disorder: Part 1

### Or

### What Goes On In Your Thoughts and Feelings

There is nothing one can say about human beings that is true all the time. However, certain personality characteristics and ways of thinking are extremely common among people who have panic attacks. You may find some of yourself in the following description:

**Parentification** (Learning As A Child How To Not Be Yourself)
People who develop panic attacks were often denied their childhoods. Yes, they were children. But often, they were

required to be something else -- usually, adults and parents. This comes about from having to be the one who always helps out - the "strong one." In other words, the person to whom everyone looks in a crisis. Often, the future person with panic was the oldest child in the family. Or, there was some other reason she became "parentified": Having to take care of ill or alcoholic parents is a common example. Another is being expected to care for much younger or disabled brothers or sisters. Or, being the homemaker while the mother or father in a single parent family went to work.

The parentified child learns to put aside what she wants to do in favor of what she is required to do. In other words, she develops a "must-oriented" way of living and behaving. She learns to do what she must, not what she wants. She makes responsibility her first priority. Many people even learn to take a kind of pleasure in this. After all, it feels pretty good to have everyone looking to you for help and direction -- especially in a crisis.

Unfortunately, the cost of being the strong one is that one is obviously not allowed to be "the weak one." Or, "the irresponsible one." Or, "the helpless or overwhelmed one." Certainly not the "playful and carefree one." So the price of always being the strong one is learning very well how to put aside being what you are in favor of being what somebody says you should be. During childhood, this costs us the experience of being children -- of having a childhood. It also engrains in us the habit of ignoring what we want and paying attention to what we feel we should do. Ultimately, we have ignored what we want so often that we barely even know what it is.

Another way that pre-agoraphobic children learn to care for others (and not be themselves) is being required by their parents to meet excessively high expectations. Having to always be on the Honor Roll at school is one example. Or having to excel at a particular sport. Pretty soon, the child learns that she "just isn't good enough" unless she takes care of her parents' needs in one way or another. (Of course, what is happening here is that the parent does not feel good herself and is looking to compensate for this by having a showpiece child.)

This situation is a trap for the child. Even if she is actually capable of doing Honor Roll level work, academic performance may just not be her interest. She has no choice, however, because she knows that she will have failed her parents if she does not perform to their expectations. So, she is stuck. And if she does not have the mental equipment to get the A's, she is in an even more impossible bind. Bottom line? She learns that who she is (being not that good at school or being uninterested in academics) is not acceptable. She is unacceptable to her parents and worse yet, since she wants them to be happy with her, she is unacceptable to herself. And here begins a lifetime habit of rejecting who she is or what she wants in favor of what others want her to be. She becomes "a professional doormat" – allowing others to walk all over her because she knows she is no good and the least she can do is try to please others who supposedly are.

This is also the reason that people with panic are the best people to have around in an emergency. They are prepared, calm and ready to meet whatever need presents itself. Just as they did as parentified children, they are ready to take care of all eventualities. This is why most such people have developed their own Emergency Kits without reading this manual. They are ready. For anything.

I can think of no finer example of this than what happened at the Second Annual Phobia Conference in Washington, D.C. The conference was attended by many hundreds of phobic people as well as many hundreds of counselors. It was held in a large, high-rise hotel. On the second day, after I had presented my paper in the assigned meeting room on the sixth floor, I entered a full elevator to go back to the general meeting on the main floor. The elevator contained many agoraphobics and perhaps one or two professionals. Believe it or not, while the elevator was going down, the worst nightmare of any person with panic occurred: all the power in the building went out! We were stuck in a dark elevator between floors with no idea how long we would be there! Surely, there would be many people having panic attacks -- right? Wrong! A number of people just dug into their bags and pulled out flashlights, food, bandages and pretty much anything else one could possibly need in that situation.

We were stuck for some 20 minutes. Then the power came on and the elevator brought us down to the first floor. Everyone was laughing and joking about whether this had been planned by someone. But there were no panic attacks. Naturally. The situation was what everyone had trained for all their lives!

This is why I have always said that in an emergency, I would want to be with no one so much as an agoraphobic.

Of course, feeling that you must be ready and able to solve every possible problem is a setup because there are lots of situations that no one can solve. This brings us to:

## The I-Can't-But-I-Must-Double-Bind
(Which is also: How To Get In A Trap All By Yourself In Your own Mind)

Learning in childhood that you must be an adult although you are only a kid develops the habit of feeling you must do something even though you can't. In other words, being in an "I-Can't-But-I-Must Double Bind" (ICBIM for short). This is a mental merry-go-round that goes as follows: "I must do this because if I don't, there will be awful consequences. But I can't do this because something (whatever it is in the particular situation) prevents me. But I must do it because... But I can't do it because... But I must do it because... etc." Here are some examples:

## Example No. 1:

I must speak at my mother's funeral because if I don't I will regret it for the rest of my life. But I can't speak at my mother's funeral because I know that as soon as I begin to talk about her I will start crying and be unable to speak. But I must speak or everyone will think I don't care. But I can't speak because I will choke up. But if I don't speak... etc. End result? Panic attack.

## Example No. 2:

Sylvia's version: I must get out of this abusive marriage because no one should put up with being beaten up. But I can't get out of the marriage because I won't be able to support the baby and she would be without a father which would scar her for life, and anyhow, I don't want to be alone. But staying in the marriage means that I'm going to get beaten up the next time he comes home drunk. But leaving the marriage means...etc.

## A further common development:

The panic attacks, themselves, become the "I can't" part of the double bind. Here's how this goes:

## Example No. 3:

I must go to my husband's office Christmas party or everyone will think his marriage is on the rocks or that I'm snubbing them. But I can't go to the office party because I might have a panic attack there and completely embarrass both him and myself. But I can't not go because:

- Everyone will think badly of me.

- Everyone will think badly of my husband.

- My husband may lose his job.

- My husband may get passed over for promotion and we'll be in financial trouble because of me.

- Everyone else is bringing their wives to the party.

But I can't go because:

- I may have to leave and all the problems from not going would be even worse.

- My having a panic attack could cause even greater problems for my husband at work.

- I could faint and make a scene.

When this happens, the Panic Disorder is really feeding upon itself. It is causing itself. The fear of having a panic attack has become the "I can't" that stands in the way of the "I musts."

Now what? Answer: Do the...

# Assignments for Chapter 5

## 1. Your Anxiety Chart.

This consists of turning the data you have been collecting in your Anxiety Diary into a graph format so that you can easily see the ups and downs you have been going through. (And a lot more.) On the next page is a sample. Also, there is a fresh copy on the following page so that you can duplicate it for your own use. Take a look at them and then go on to the explanation of what they mean and how to create your own. (You can print out larger versions of these charts at http://agoraphobia-treatment.com/AnxietyCharts.pdf).

Anxiety Chart

# Anxiety Chart

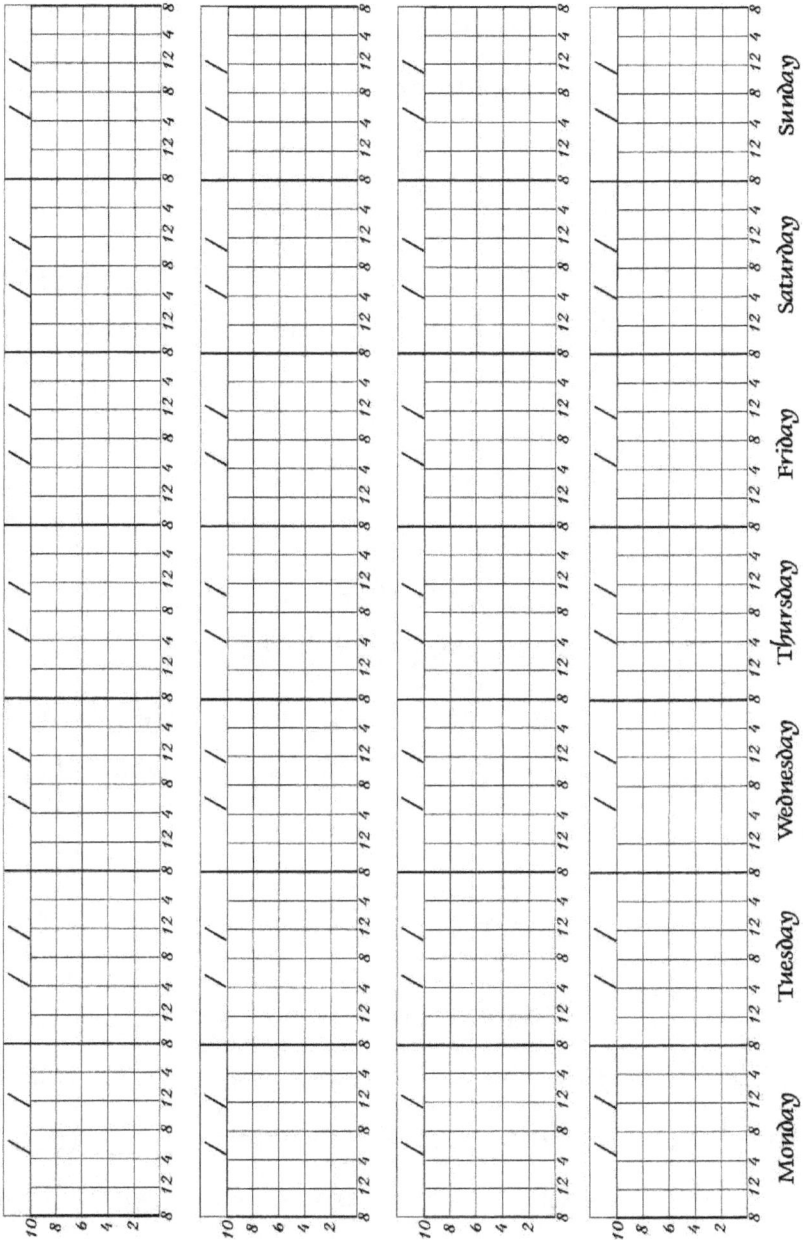

| | Monday | Tuesday | Wednesday | Thursday | Friday | Saturday | Sunday |

As you look at the chart itself, you see that there are four rows of boxes with the numbers "8, 12, 4, 8, 12, 4" repeating underneath them. These numbers represent 8 A.M., Noon, 4 P.M., 8 P.M., Midnight and 4 A.M. They keep repeating across the page so that there are 7 sets of them per row. Thus, each row represents one week. Since there are 4 rows on the sheet, you can chart 4 weeks' worth of days. The days of the week are shown at the bottom and there are spaces above for you to write in the date as has been done for the first four days of this sample.

Going up the left side of the chart are the numbers "2, 4, 6, 8 and 10." These represent the severity of your anxiety. Ten is reserved for the worst anxiety of which you are capable. Zero is none. So an 8 is pretty close to the max. 2 is pretty low-level anxiety. And so on.

Now let's look at the sample chart:

You start off on Monday, Dec. 2, 2002 with no anxiety at 8 A.M. This lasts until the kids get home for lunch at noon. They remind you that the school Christmas Show (that you promised to attend) is coming up in one week. This raises your anxiety level to a 3. As you watch the soaps and work on dinner, it drops down to a level of 1 by about 2 P.M. (2 P.M. is represented on the time scale as halfway between noon and 4

P.M.) In your diary, you write something like: "12/2/02, Noon: Reminded of Christmas Show."

You stay at a 1 during your kids and husband coming home and through the evening until after the children are in bed. About 10 P.M., while you are sitting with your husband in the living room, he announces that he has decided that you and he should have another child. Your anxiety zooms up to an 8 and stays up there for an hour or two while the two of you "discuss" it. You are looking at a fear-filled pregnancy because you are nearing 40, nights without sleep as he does not help with getting up to change and feed the baby, stretching an already overstretched budget to support a fourth child and all the panic attacks this will entail. He is looking at how nice it would be if the baby were finally a boy and he had a son to do guy things with and to carry on the family name. In your diary, you write: "10 P.M.: Jerry announces he wants another child."

By about midnight, your anxiety has only decreased to a 6. And you stay at this level until you (sort of) fall asleep from 3 A.M. until about 7 A.M. You rate your fitful sleep anxiety level at a little less than the 6 and it goes back to the 6 as soon as you get up. During the day, you chart these anxiety levels (as shown in the sample) while your 6 continues. However, sometime in the afternoon, it occurs to you to pull out this book to see if it has anything to say to you. As you read, it comes home to you that having another child would be not just one, but a whole series of traps for you. And you realize that all the anxiety you are experiencing is telling you something – you really do not want to do this. So after chewing on this a while, you decide that you are just going to have to put your foot down and say "no" and that's that.

This decision lowers your anxiety to about a 3 by 4 P.M. but you know it's not going to be easy. That night (Tuesday, 12/3/02) around 8 P.M., you send the girls upstairs, swallow hard and go for it. This, of course, sends your anxiety up to a 7. You and Jerry thrash your way through it, and he finally gets it. Even though he's disappointed, he says he can see that it wouldn't be the best idea – especially for you. Your anxiety goes down to a 3 and remains there until you get up at 6 A.M. It goes up to a 4 because of your worry that Jerry will have changed his mind or there will be some fall out. But no, all seems okay as he goes off to work. Your anxiety level goes to a 1 and here you are at 7 P.M. on Wednesday, 12/4/02, noting that it stayed there all day and recording in your diary what happened.

Now go ahead and graph the data in your actual Anxiety Diary onto the blank Anxiety Chart.

The bang for your buck:

The payoff for the relatively small effort of keeping your Anxiety Chart and Diary is enormous. As discussed in Chapter 2, I have found over and over again that if we want to change something, the first thing we need to do is pay close attention to it. We need to learn everything there is to know about it. The Anxiety Diary and Chart let you see how much anxiety you are really experiencing and for how long. You may be surprised. There may be a lot less anxiety than you think. Also, they show you what is happening to your overall anxiety levels for periods of weeks to months. This allows you to try out the various therapy techniques and see the effects they are having on your general level of anxiety. It is very encouraging as you can look at 4 weeks' worth of effort and see how there may be ups and downs, but the overall trend is definitely going in the right direction.

Keep both the Anxiety Diary and Anxiety Chart going from now on. If there are not many changes in your anxiety level throughout the day, you may do them once a day. Before going to bed can be a good time because it will be a way of looking over the day and taking stock of how you are coming along. (There is more about making use of these in Chapter 11.)

## 2. I-Can't-But-I-Must Double Binds

Write down 5 of these that you recall getting into. If you are in any right now, these are the best ones to note. Write all the reasons that you can't do whatever it is and then write down all the reasons you must do it. Start a running journal of these in your notebook and add to it each time you get in a new ICBIM double bind. Keep track of what became of the ones that are past.

## 3. Continue taking Field Trips

Get a momentum going of getting out each week with your program partners or with friends. Go to new places – even if it is just a park that you rarely visit ½ mile from your home.

# CHAPTER SIX

---

# The Psychology of Panic Disorder: Part 2

## Or

## More Thoughts and Feelings

---

### Catastrophic Thinking and Anticipatory Anxiety

(In other words: Living Through Disasters Before They Happen)

The world abounds with "I-Can't-But-I-Must" double-binds. And, as you know all so well, many of them involve the belief that you "must" not have a panic attack in this or that place. "What if I have a panic attack in a restaurant and faint right there in front of everybody?" "What if I have a panic attack while driving and lose control of the car and injure or kill everybody?" "What if I make a fool of myself?" "What if people see that I have this ridiculous condition of not being able to go into a grocery store?" "What if I get stuck somewhere and can't get back home?" And on and on -- you know the drill.

This fear of having a panic attack or of something else terrible happening is called **"Catastrophic Thinking"** or **"Catastrophizing."** In other words, it is the process of thinking up catastrophes. Some people call these thoughts the "What-Ifs."

When we think this way, we make ourselves anxious. This is called **"Anticipatory Anxiety."** That is – the anxiety one feels in anticipation of something awful happening. Many people with panic are aware of this process and refer to it when they talk about the panic attacks "I worked myself into."

It is very natural to fear panic attacks. One of the characters on M*A*S*H once said: "I hate being scared -- it terrifies me." This is true. We not only have the panic attacks, but we have the fear of having panic attacks. And panic attacks are frightening. The "fight-or-flight response" that we have as a result of all the adrenalin pouring into our systems causes us to feel that something terrible must be happening. In fact, one study found that people having anxiety or panic accounted for 50 percent of all first visits to cardiologists. It feels terrible. No doubt about it. So people who have panic get "a double whammy" – the panic attacks themselves plus the Anticipatory Anxiety.

Actually, the Anticipatory Anxiety is often a bigger problem than the anxiety of the panic attacks. This came home to me in the first year of my residency – some forty years ago. I was seeing a patient who had panic attacks while driving on the highway to work. He would develop the feeling that a wall of fog was following just behind his car and that he was therefore cut off from the rest of the world. Also, this caused him to feel that he couldn't go back since the world behind him was sort of erased by the fog as he went. These thoughts and feelings would escalate until he had a panic attack.

My teachers and I did not know much about Agoraphobia in those days (for instance, I hadn't discovered The Key) and my patient and I were getting nowhere towards ridding him of the panic attacks. Finally, in desperation, I asked him how long the panic attacks lasted. He said about 20 minutes usually. Then I asked how often he had them. He answered once or twice a week. When I realized that he was out of work and in a psychiatric hospital because of his fear of what he experienced 40 minutes a week, I was shocked. "Do you mean to say," I asked, "that your whole life, 24 hours a day, 7 days a week has been messed up because of your feelings about what you go through for 40 minutes a week?!!" He agreed that this was so. "Well," I said. "We do not seem to be getting anywhere about changing those forty minutes, but what if you changed all the rest of the minutes? What if you went back home and back to work with the conclusion that we had failed? That you were going to go through forty horrible minutes each week and nothing was going to change that. But you could at least have the rest of the time each week to live your life?"

Well, this made sense to him so we agreed that he would try it: He would expect the forty minutes of panic attacks each week but would try to not let it affect the rest of his week any more than necessary. And he was able to do it pretty well. I did not know him long enough to hear whether this reduced his panic attacks. From what I know now, I think it probably did. But the last I did hear, he was back enjoying the most of his life and feeling good about it.

I never forgot the moral to this story: *sometimes peoples' reactions to a problem are bigger problems than the original problem, itself.* (We frequently see this same phenomenon in physical medicine. For example, that's what is happening in severe allergic reactions.) Later, when I specialized in the treatment of Panic Disorders, I found that my experience with this patient had been typical – the Anticipatory Anxiety is often a much more debilitating problem than the panic attacks the anxiety is about! Also, as in the case of this patient, it is quite treatable.

## Displacement

(Transferring Feelings From What They Are About To Something Else)

The way being trapped in our lives becomes fear of being trapped in places such as the grocery store is the process of "displacement." It is a psychological phenomenon that has long been recognized. In fact, Freud first described it. Here's how it works:

We believe that there is nothing we can do about the Life Trap so we stop thinking about it. But it's as though there is somebody within us trying to give us signals that something is very wrong. The signals are the panic attacks in trapped situations in daily life. That not-so-little voice (of the panic attack) is constantly saying: "You've got to get out of this trap!" The big trap, which we feel we can do nothing about, gets experienced as all these little Day-to-Day Traps. In other words, the feelings of fear have been displaced (moved from one place to another) from the big trap to the little ones.

Perhaps you remember some of the old cartoons in which the character gets hit on the head causing a bump to arise. He pushes it down with his hand only to have another bump come up some place else. I am often reminded of this when thinking of displacement because we try to ignore the feelings of one trap only to have those same feelings come out about another trap.

As we already noted, there can be some benefit to this. Being unable to go to the grocery store by yourself may result in your husband doing more of his fair share of the shopping. Or, accompanying you to the store may give him a way to be caring which he didn't have before. This brings us to...

## Primary and Secondary Gain

For those who are interested, this after-the-fact benefit of panic attacks is what has been called "secondary gain." In other words, it is a secondary benefit from the way of adapting that we call "panic attacks."

When I first started working with Panic Disorder and Agoraphobia, there were very few professionals who recognized what it was. The poor patients of those days got all sorts of wrong diagnoses and treatments (like my guy with the following fog who had admitted himself to a hospital).

Frequently, agoraphobics were considered to be highly dependent people because they relied upon others to either help them go places or to go places for them. Some counselors got the idea that maybe this reliance upon others was the purpose of developing Agoraphobia in the first place. In other words, agoraphobics were simply getting others to do for them.

Wrong! Anything good that comes out of agoraphobics' reliance upon others is simply a side effect. Or, "secondary gain." The primary "gain" is that it is the mind's way of dealing with seemingly impossible circumstances -- namely, traps. People with panic cannot get out of their traps or (often) even afford to experience them as such. So instead, the fear is displaced onto the little Day-to-Day traps that can be successfully dealt with by avoiding them. That is the primary gain (or reason) for Agoraphobia - it is a way to deal with an impossible situation.

Can you see why, towards the end of treatment, many agoraphobics come to realize that home -- which had been considered the only "safe place", was really the only unsafe place? When this happens, the displacement has been undone. And the person is experiencing her Life Trap for what it really is. Then it can be dealt with -- no matter how hard that may be. Also, ceasing to project her anger gives her the assertiveness to stand up for her right to an untrapped life. (Huh? Don't worry. Read on.)

**Projection** (Ascribing your feelings to the other guy.)

This is the phenomenon of believing that someone else has feelings or thoughts that are actually feelings you are having but of which you are not aware. (Whew! <u>That</u> was complicated.) But projection is really quite simple. It is thinking the other person has your feelings. Instead of knowing you have them.

Here's an example: I perceive you as being mad at me. You, in fact, are not mad at me. Where did I get the mistaken idea? From myself. Where else <u>could</u> it have originated? There are only the two of us here.

So, the idea of being angry came from me and I put it on you. Did I know I was doing this? Of course not! If I had known the anger was in me, not in you, I would not have perceived you as angry. I could only have made this mistake if I didn't know it <u>was</u> a mistake. In other words, the projection of anger onto you was an unconscious process. It happens without our knowing it. And projection always is unconscious. As soon as we become aware that we are projecting, we aren't doing it anymore.

Also, we are projecting all the time. In fact, it is how we see the whole world. Sometimes our projections are true. Sometimes they are not. And sometimes, we will never know.

You say: "This is great chocolate!" And I say: "I know what you mean." I am projecting. In actual fact, I will never know if the chocolate tastes the same to you as it does to me. All I can do is project onto you how it tastes to me and imagine that that is what you are experiencing. I assume the projection is accurate. But there is no way to know because I cannot get inside you to know what it is like to get the chocolate sensations from your taste buds.

Lots of times, it is clear that our projections are untrue. He says: "Isn't that a beautiful green?" She says: "I think it's awful!" He thought she would see it as beautiful. His projection onto her of how the green looks to him was wrong. It does not look that way to her.

Freud realized that the processes of projection and displacement are how a phobia gets born. The famous "Little Hans" case illustrated this. Little Hans had a phobia of horses. Freud figured out that this fear came about because Little

Hans was angry with his father. You cannot want to overthrow the king for very long before you begin to believe that the king might not like this and has it in for you in return. In other words, you project your anger onto him. (The fact of the matter could be that the king doesn't even know you exist off in your remote corner of the kingdom.)

So Little Hans projected his anger onto his father, perceiving that it was not he who was angry with his father but that it was his father who was angry with him.

Living in a house with a big adult who you think is angry with you was too scary for Little Hans to deal with. So Little Hans' mind solved the problem for him (of course, without Little Hans knowing about it) by displacing the fear <u>from</u> his father <u>onto</u> horses (which were the common means of transportation at the time). Now Little Hans had a fear he could deal with. As long as he ran away and hid whenever a horse came down the street, Little Hans felt safe. And voila – a phobia was born.

It all starts with projection – in this case, thinking that someone else has evil designs towards you when it is really you who has the evil designs towards them.

This may all seem to be an unnecessary complication - something for psychoanalysts to worry about, not regular people. And it's true that you don't have to understand it to overcome your Panic Disorder. But it gets right back to the world of "regular people" if you happen to realize that an unfelt anger at someone is what started one of your fears.

Where does Sylvia's fear come from? Not from Darrell's threats or even his abuse. She is used to those. They do not frighten her, they just hurt. *But they make her mad!* And, like Little Hans, there is nothing she can do about her anger. So, she projects it and then displaces it onto the grocery store situation. If Sylvia realized how angry she is at Darrell and at her father, her fears would largely vanish! Just like that. *Anger felt equals fear dissolved.*

## Depression and Panic

As mentioned in Chapter 1, the prevalence of depression is greater than 50% at one time or another in the agoraphobic's lifetime. This makes perfect sense since depression is so closely linked to anger. You have probably heard the old saw that "depression is anger turned inward." Well, that is rather an oversimplification but it does contain the truth that depression often results from how an individual deals with anger. When anger is not acceptable to you and you cannot allow yourself to feel angry, then a phobia can result just as we saw with Little Hans. Or depression can result.

Here's how I came to understand this: I noticed that many situations that cause anxiety for other people were like the exams I faced in college causing anxiety for me. The catastrophic thoughts I had about failing included the ideas that I (totally) would be a failure, that I could not face my friends or parents if I flunked out of school and that I would end up in some kind of humiliating job. In other words, it was as though I had constructed a kind of paper mache model of myself that I constantly kept an eye on to make sure that it was good enough. The anxiety over possibly failing the exam was the fear that my image would be permanently disfigured. I would look at it and see that it was bad (a failure, humiliating job, etc.)

Furthermore, I noticed that if enough time went by, my anxiety would turn into depression. After struggling and struggling to master all the material for the exam and finding that it was impossible, I would stop fearing that I would fail the exam and, instead, conclude that failure was inevitable. I gave up. There was no longer any anxiety because failure had really already happened. I just had yet to go through the exam and finally get my grade. But the fact that it was going to be an 'F' was already settled. So my paper mache image became an image of a bad me and there was nothing I could do about it. In other words, *anxiety was the fear that I would have to conclude that I was no good, and depression was having already concluded it.*

After noticing this (many years later, unfortunately), I began looking at other situations in which people felt anxious to see if this was generally the case. I found that it often was. For instance, the fear of having a panic attack and being judged as crazy by others is nothing more than the fear that your image of yourself will be: "a person who others think is crazy." So it is that image, once again, that is damaged.

Try it yourself: Think of your catastrophic thoughts. See if the catastrophes are not really about your image becoming something you feel badly about. Then, think about your depressed thoughts. Again, are they not about the conclusion that some bad image you feared seeing as you has already happened – that you <u>are</u> that image?

So it becomes obvious what will occur if you feel angry and, at the same time, feel that it is bad to be angry or to be seen as angry. You will have anxiety that the anger will come out or be perceived by others. This would turn that image into a bad one. ("She's an angry person.") Eventually, you will conclude that you <u>are</u> that bad image anyway; because the anger doesn't go away – it just stays and shows people that you are that angry (bad) person. At this point, your anxiety turns into depression.

Lastly, it is worth noting that anxiety and depression seem to be alternatives. If you become depressed, your anxiety goes down. This makes sense. If anxiety is the fear that you will conclude you are bad and depression is having concluded it, then of course you will only have one or the other. You will not fear something happening if you have concluded that it has already happened. Just like when I became depressed about the hopelessness of passing the exam – instantly, I was no longer anxious about taking it. (Ugh! What a lot of stress that was for nothing!)

# Assignments for Chapter 6

## 1. Write Out The Catastrophes

Get out all those catastrophes now! Sit down with your notebook. Pick on something that you do not have a problem with doing. Pretend that you do have a problem with it and are facing having to do it. Write down every catastrophic thought that a person could have about doing it. Do this again about something else. And another something else until you run out of catastrophes. If you think of any more catastrophes later, add them to your list.

## 2. Displacement

Write down 5 examples of displacement. Use your own or others' real life displacements if you can.

## 3. Projection

Write down 10 examples of projection. For this, you should have no trouble thinking of real life examples.

## 4. Traps and Anger

Examine one of your traps – especially a Life Trap. See if you can identify where you are really angry about something at the heart of it all.

## 5. Anxiety Diary and Chart

Continue your Anxiety Diary and Chart.

## 6. Field Trips

Continue taking Field Trips. You might try a visit to a small town museum – you can learn surprisingly interesting things.

# CHAPTER SEVEN

---

## Therapy

## Or

## How To Solve It

---

For the next several chapters, we will first look at the use of medications and then go into methods from three major forms of therapy that work to overcome Panic Disorder and Agoraphobia. How do I know they work? Easy. Because I have seen them do so over and over. (There is also a convincing body of medical research proving that they work.)

No single therapy seems to do it all for everyone. So when working with someone, I combine the therapies to fit the needs of that person. When one works better for someone, I use that kind the most. And I add in some of what I have learned from some less common forms of therapy as fits the

---

situation. Most often, I also teach people how to do meditation. So this will be covered, too.

I believe that people can go quite far with applying these methods for themselves. They are not complicated. Mostly, making them work takes sticking with it. In this chapter, we'll start by going over some general principles about therapies and how to use them.

## Principle 1:

A very wise teacher said: "Each person must work out her own salvation diligently." In other words, by using the methods I will be describing, you can get past your Panic Disorder. But, there's a "but." And the "but" is that you must adapt the techniques to your own self and your own ways of making changes.

In order to quit smoking, I had read all sorts of methods and helpful ways of going about it. But, in the end, I found that I had to work out my own way of using those methods and even invent some new variations to make it. Some methods were not for me at all. Others were crucial.

## Principle 2:

*You have to do it.* Just reading about how to make changes will be as effective as reading about how to play the piano. I had one very bright college student in one of my treatment groups. She dealt with what she was taught in exactly the same way that she treated her courses in college: She quickly learned all the principles and could quote them back to me without a moment's hesitation. In fact, her understanding was so good that she could tell other members of the group how to apply the techniques to their own situations and how to get over obstacles when these arose. Of course, she never actually *did* the techniques herself. What was the need? She understood what had been presented perfectly.

Naturally, the moral of the story is that she completed the program with the ability to get an A+ on any exam on the subject but having no fewer panic attacks than she had to begin with. And the poor, dumb, average person who hadn't caught on nearly as quickly but who went out and *actually used* what she learned, had achieved all sorts of successes.

We had nagged and warned and predicted that this was going to happen if she did not put the techniques into practice, but that was one lesson she somehow did not get. Or, maybe did not want to get. And she went off telling herself that the fault was in the treatment methods, still not having learned the one lesson that would have served her so well in this and many other areas of her life. I mentioned before the saying that the only experiences that are failures are those we do not learn from. That was certainly true for my college student. There was a lesson in her having failed to overcome her Panic Disorder. And if she had learned that one, it might have turned out to be even more valuable to her than having succeeded in overcoming Panic.

So, try out all the methods. Understanding them won't get rid of panic attacks. Doing them will. Then, work out your own salvation by adapting them to your needs and creating variations that work for you. Experiment! This is vital! Once you start treating your panics and reactions in an experimental way ("Gee, I wonder what will happen if I try this…"), you have the attitude that makes things change.

## Principle 3:

**Keep at it.** Do not discard a method just because it does not seem to produce results right away. This is work! (Although it is also fun, at times.) Do not take one or two piano lessons and give up because you are not able to give concerts. Each of the methods works. If one is not working for you, you are just not yet skilled enough in using it. But you will be that skilled with practice. Anyone can learn and use them. After you have learned how to make a particular method work, you can decide whether this is one you want to use more or less than others.

## Principle 4:

**Master each technique the way it is given.** Once you get it to work, then modify it to your own style if you want. Some of the methods may be unpleasant for you. Do them anyway. They will work. And they may become your best friends. Later on, you can emphasize some other techniques if you want. Do not try to invent your own therapy as you go. It would be too easy to indulge in just skipping the hard parts and getting nowhere as a result.

## Principle 5:

As was mentioned in the Assignments for Chapter 1, other people with similar problems can be a great help. Especially if you get stuck. Lots of people have been through this or are working their way out of it. There are many groups for people with this problem – self-help groups, groups led by trained therapists and others. It is very useful to share your experiences with other people, hear about their similar struggles and successes and get tips for getting over humps in the road. When you do the assignments for getting out in the world, it is much more fun to have someone (or ones) to do them with. Other members of your group would be ideal for this.

If a therapist runs the group, her approach may or may not be compatible with the program you are following here. Since these are mainstream methods, they will fit quite well with most therapy groups. However, if you encounter a conflict, you will need to decide which way you want to go. Most places, there are lots of other options of groups if you decide to continue with this rather than switch horses. Also, as you doubtless know, the Internet is full of resources for finding groups or others with whom to talk.

One caveat: I have known groups in which the members are not working to overcome their Panic. They are usually leaderless support groups and the aim of the people who run them is mutual misery-sharing. The members are going nowhere with their problem nor are they seeking to. They have given up. There is an underlying belief in these groups that Panic is incurable. So the members' goal is simply to hold each others' hands while living their unhappy lives.

As if this were not bad enough, people in these groups are often getting worse by the process of "symptom-swapping."

This phenomenon occurs in all groups but especially in these going-nowhere groups. It is exactly what the name implies – people pick up each others' symptoms. Somebody in the group talks about seeing flashing lights during a panic attack and pretty soon, you are having flashing lights in yours. (Stop it! I used that example on purpose. Flashing lights is not a symptom of panic attacks so drop it!)

Support groups in which people are just helping each other make the best of a bad thing are fine for diabetes, schizophrenia and having one leg. When it comes to panic attacks, however, they are simply well intentioned barriers to recovery.

## Principle 6 – Getting Help:

Besides working this program with help and supervision by an appropriately-trained professional, if you get stuck or simply wish to work that way, you can enter individual therapy. But there's a difficulty: How do you find a good therapist? Here are some suggestions:

1. Get a recommendation from someone you know and trust. Preferably from a number of people. And preferably, people with problems like yours. If you attend a group, you may get good leads there. Checking out a therapist on an internet doctor rating site should be done with caution, however. Often, the only people to give a rating do so because they are unhappy about something and this gives them an opportunity to blow off steam. The first version of this book got all 5-star ratings except for one 1-star. I couldn't imagine what book that individual had read - his statements about it were so far off. But some people took what he said as gospel, didn't get the book and never got to see the benefits that those 5-star raters had found.

2. Ask the therapist what her credentials are. I know this can take assertiveness and that may be a problem area for you, but it's good practice and can have important results.

   Therapists come with all kinds and amounts of training. In fact, guess what is often required of you in order to call yourself a therapist or to offer "counseling"? Nothing! That's right – nothing. And guess what a bunch of high-faluting sounding initials after your name can mean? Again, nothing. Or they can mean that you attended a two-day workshop from God-knows-who and received a certificate when you woke up at the end because you paid the fee. Giving workshops and certificates of attendance is big business. Do you know what a Certified Agoraphobia Counseling Associate is? It's a C.A.C.A.

The point is that different states regulate the use of some words and not others. In some states, you will have to have certain training and/or take an exam to call yourself a "psychotherapist," and in other states, you won't. Initials can mean a lot or nothing at all. The only way to know is to call up the state licensing board and ask (unless you are able to ask the therapist, herself).

Certain degrees and titles are always regulated. M.S.W. always means that the person has a Masters of Social Work degree. To get this degree, the individual has to have graduated from a Masters program in Social Work. Usually, such programs are 2-year post-graduate degree programs that one enters after getting a 4-year Bachelor's degree. The amount of training and experience doing therapy is quite variable in such programs. Some schools of social work are known for their excellent training in doing therapy. Others focus more on other issues.

Psychiatrists must have a M.D. degree plus 3 years of specialty training in Psychiatry. This is a legal requirement for someone to call herself a Psychiatrist. Again, training programs differ but all Psychiatrists are trained in prescribing medications and in some forms of psychotherapy. They are permitted to call themselves "Doctor." They are physicians – namely, Doctors of Medicine.

People who have majored in Psychology in college or graduate school can call themselves "Psychologists." Thus, they may have 4 years of post-high school education, 6 years, 9 years or more. They may have Bachelor's degrees, Master's or Ph.D.'s. Ph.D. Psychologists may also call themselves "Doctor." They may have as many or more years of specialty training in Psychology as a Psychiatrist has in Psychiatry. Their title of "Doctor" refers to being a "Doctor of Philosophy."

One is not necessarily better than the other. But they are different. Only Psychologists are permitted to administer psychological testing. In most states, only M.D.'s can prescribe medications. (Although many states are increasingly licensing certain Psychologists and others with special training to prescribe also – such as Psychiatric Nurse Practitioners.) Some Psychologists have more training in doing therapy than the average Psychiatrist.

Some have much less. You need to ask a Psychologist what her degree is and what is her experience in doing therapy.

For professionals who are not newly graduated, the most important factor will be the kind of work they have been doing since school. If they have been primarily doing therapy and come well recommended, they likely are a good choice. If a Psychiatrist or Psychologist has mostly been doing other work than therapy – such as research or evaluations – she may not have the skills you are after.

People with other degrees than these can be excellent therapists. But so can your hairdresser. What their training was just will not give you that information.

3.  Find out where the therapist "is coming from." Some Psychiatrists believe that medication is crucial (see "The Infamous Chemical Imbalance" in Chapter 8). So, you also need to ask what is the "orientation" of the therapist. This means what is the major kind of treatment she offers.

Although the asking may be difficult, it can also be quite revealing. If you are made to feel stupid for asking, that tells you one of the ways that person is going to make you feel in therapy. Do you want to hire someone who makes you feel stupid and pay them a lot of money to help with your problems? Better than just going away is to tell her that she made you feel stupid for asking. Now you will get to the real nitty gritty! If she tells you that that was not her intention and reassures you that you asked a legitimate question, then you will know you can talk with her. If she acts "huffy" and makes you feel that feeling stupid is one of your problems, then you also know what to expect in the future.

If the therapist tells you her orientation is towards some kind of therapy you do not really know about, ask what that is. Again, you will learn a lot.

For instance, many therapists I know seem to feel it is a good idea to answer questions by giving out the least possible amount of specific information. They seem to have really practiced saying words that leave you thinking: "Huh?? What did she say?" Are you up against one of these? Do you mind getting "put off" answers? I do.

Or, you may find out that this person really feels that your Agoraphobia is a problem with your relationship with God. Maybe that's right down your alley. Maybe not. But now you know.

4.  Finally, use your own common sense. You are the consumer. In fact, many mental health centers now refer to the people who come for treatment as "consumers," not

patients or clients. So, if you feel that you are not getting what you are after, tell your therapist. If things cannot be worked out so that you feel satisfied, switch to another therapist. Do not "throw good money after bad," as the saying goes.

I know someone who went through four years of psychoanalysis, going five days a week. The cost was enormous. He was unhappy with what he was getting, but always figured it was his fault. After all, his psychoanalyst was one of the most high-ranking in the country. Finally, he quit. He used the excuse that he was moving. Years later, another analyst who had been one of his teachers said: "I wondered how long it was going to take you to find out about him."

This does **not** mean that you should quit as soon as you and your therapist disagree about something. There are always rough spots in any relationship. In therapy, these can be the best opportunities to learn something valuable. And you do not want to be switching from therapist to therapist, always leaving just when you could have gotten something you really wanted. But if you have given it a good try with a therapist and it's not getting you anywhere, then shake the dust from your feet and move on.

Perhaps some kind of rule of thumb would be helpful: If pressed, I would say that if you felt good enough about a therapist to try it with her and you still felt you were getting nowhere after 8 sessions (or 2 months of weekly meetings), it's time to seriously consider changing.

So much for therapists. Next, we will look at medications. Then we will get to the heart of it all.

# Assignments for Chapter 7

## 1. Therapy is about change

We all have developed endless habits. We brush our teeth in the same order every time. We never eat or drink certain foods (e.g. Postum). We always wear the same kinds of clothing for casual and going out. We may wait until we have crammed in the last possible spoon before running the dishwasher. We are slobs or neatniks. We bathe every so many days. We go through the same ritual before bed each night. We never throw things out or we get rid of everything we can. We listen to the same music and watch the same TV shows. Every minute, we are engaging in some habit. This assignment is to do 3 things differently from normal each day. See if you find some changes you'd like to make permanent.

## 2. Continue your Anxiety Diary and Chart

## 3. Continue your Field Trips

This week, you might try a store you have never been to.

## 4. Keep up your "Traps" diary from Chapter 4

# CHAPTER EIGHT

## Medications

### Or

### Is There Better Living Through Chemistry?

Medications are an increasingly popular way that people deal with their problems nowadays. It seems that everybody is in favor of them. We are in an age when medical research is constantly making new discoveries about various functions of the brain and brain chemicals. There are many Psychiatrists who believe that physical and chemical processes going on in the brain will eventually go far towards explaining the causes of emotional problems. Consequently, it makes sense to them to use physical means (medications) to correct those problems.

Also, medications are an easy fix (when they work). You simply take the pills as directed. You don't have to change your lifestyle or your way of handling situations. And the side effects you have to put up with are becoming less and less onerous as new, higher-tech medications are being developed.

Naturally, the drug companies doing the developing want you to use their medications to deal with your problems. It is such big business that people who follow the stock market usually know all about new drugs under development long before the physicians who will be doing the prescribing have even heard of them. This is also why the drug companies in recent years have begun to direct their advertising at the general public. Even on primetime TV, we are assailed by ads asking whether we have this, that and the other symptoms, telling us we might well have depression, sinus trouble or ugly toenails and advising us to ask our doctors about prescribing their drug. (Interestingly, this is illegal in many other countries.)

Lastly, the insurance companies want us to use medications to deal with our problems. They cost the company a whole lot less than seeing a therapist. So the insurance industry encourages them by limiting coverage for therapy while paying more of the cost of medications.

So why shouldn't you just take that pill and be done with it? Well, maybe you should. But here are some things worth considering before you toss this book in the circular file and start looking for someone with a prescription pad:

First, taking that pill may well <u>not</u> mean that you are done with it. To be approved for treatment of panic attacks, there has to be research showing that the drug is statistically significantly more effective than a placebo (sugar pill). It doesn't have to work in everybody – no drug does. Nor does it have to get rid of all your panic attacks when it does work – it just has to lessen them significantly. So, if you decide to go with medications as at least part of your program, you should be aware that they may not work completely and that you may have to try a number of them to find the one that gives you the most effect.

Second, another reason the pill may not leave you done with the problem is that the panic attacks come back after you stop taking the medication. In certain research projects, the panic attacks did not return in some people (for as long as the study lasted). But even in those studies, many other people had to stay on the medication for life if they wanted the effect to remain.

This makes sense to me because the medication has not changed the cause of the panic attacks (traps). So, if the medication is simply blocking the *effect* of the trap (panic attacks), naturally that effect will return as soon as the block is removed. If, however, the individual got out of her trap while taking the medication, then of course the panic attacks will not return after stopping it. (Until the next trap.)

This situation of medications not curing a problem is common throughout medicine and psychiatry. Recommending that a medication be taken for life is frequently done for Depression, Bipolar Disorder, Schizophrenia, ADHD, some Anxiety Disorders and many other conditions. Naturally. Despite all the research, books and excitement going on about "the biological basis of psychiatric disorders", the field of medicine is a long, long way from defining a clear biological cause for even one of these conditions. Much less finding a drug that will correct that cause and leave it corrected.

When I was in medical school, one of my professors made this point by challenging us to name three conditions that could be cured (meaning the root cause corrected) other than by antibiotics or surgery. (Nowadays, I suppose one could add antiviral and antifungal medications as well.) We couldn't. And that was his point. Possibly gene-based medicine will change this situation but we are running into a lot of complications there, too.

Generally, medications only work as long as we take them. Lipid-lowering drugs improve cholesterol as long as we take them. Diuretics, antacids, analgesics and nose drops all work only as long as we take them.

Meanwhile, non-medication treatments for the milder emotional disorders have often been shown to be at least as effective as medications and more long-lasting. There have been studies with this result on phobias, depression, obsessive-compulsive disorder and even insomnia.

The third reason you may not want to put all your eggs in the medication basket is side effects. Even though the drug companies are always working to take the market away from each other by finding drugs with fewer side effects, and even though they are making progress, all medications do have side effects. Just as the strength of the desired effect of a drug (fewer panic attacks) varies from one person to another, so do the side effects. An agoraphobic friend may have no problem taking a particular medication but when you take it, your sex life goes down the drain. (This is a common side effect of Prozac-like drugs.) Whenever we take any medication, we have to weigh the positives and negatives. Sometimes the choice is clear-cut. Other times, the benefits may not be so pronounced and the side effects may be considerable.

Fourth, no growth happens from taking a medication. Like most other therapists, I have found that problems such as Panic are signals that there is some growing to be done. By doing this growing, the panic-sufferer will not only achieve relief from panic attacks, but she will also attain a richer and happier life. I have known many ex-patients who regard their Panic as the best thing that ever happened to them because in seeking the answer to it, they found far better lives than they would ever have had otherwise. Of course! Is there any comparison between Sylvia taking a medication to stop her panic attacks and Sylvia recognizing and breaking out of her unhappy lifestyle to stop them?

The bottom line for me is that medications for Panic and Agoraphobia are okay if you want to use them while you are working your program. (Kind of like using the nicotine patch while you are stopping smoking.) But your Panic is telling you that your life can be and needs to be improved. And if you miss out on this, then for my money, you've made a poor bargain. (Reading this over, I can't resist mentioning that the guy who gave the book a 1-star rating complained that it recommended taking medications!)

Some people will say that they've been told they have to take medications because their Panic means they have...

## The Infamous Chemical Imbalance!!

- a term that has cost me a lot of time straightening out the wrong impressions it creates.

Here's how it came about: Somewhere back in the dim recesses of early therapy, people got to feeling criticized and put down for having emotional problems. All sorts of stigma developed as though it was the patients' fault. (Also, mothers were getting blamed a lot.) To say people were "mental" or "crazy" was a way to sneer at them. Generally, if you suffered from a physical illness, this did not happen to you. People did not sneer if you had pneumonia. (Although there was some of this, too – like calling a crippled person "a gimp.")

As medications for mental conditions began to be developed, some well-meaning doctors began telling their patients that they shouldn't feel embarrassed about their problems because they had "a chemical imbalance." The usual comparison was to the fact that having diabetes means you have too little insulin and you wouldn't feel guilty about that, right?

I think they had two reasons for saying this: First, they wanted to relieve the guilt and stigma, which would not only make patients feel better, but would make it easier to work out their problems. Second, they figured that something chemical had to be going on if a chemical (the medication) changed other chemicals which changed the symptoms.

So far, so good. There are chemical things going on and it is not your fault that you have your problems – you certainly did not choose them. Furthermore, feeling guilty about your problems only gets in the way of solving them.

Unfortunately, as the term "chemical imbalance" spread, it took on meanings that are not true. One of these is that your condition is a chemical imbalance. In other words, that your problem is that you have too much or too little of a particular chemical. This is not a strange thing to understand from being told: "You have a chemical imbalance." But it is *not true*!! We don't know that you have too much or too little of a particular chemical. In fact, diabetes is one of the very few conditions where we thought we do know that. (And actually, diabetes is also a lot more complicated.)

Although you may have been told that you have a chemical imbalance, no chemical has been identified as being the cause of Panic. (Yes, some drugs that affect Serotonin sometimes help with Panic. But so do some drugs that don't affect Serotonin. And sometimes one drug that affects Serotonin does not help while another does. So we certainly cannot say that Serotonin is the cause of Panic. And the same holds true for any other chemical you care to name.)

So being told that you have a chemical imbalance should not be taken to mean that it is anywhere near to being established that Panic or Agoraphobia are conditions of certain chemicals being out of whack. Some people may suspect that they are but the evidence for their suspicion is highly debatable. Not to mention the fact that panic attacks go away when people get out of their traps or when they stop working their way into them by means of catastrophic thinking.

Another false idea derived from the chemical imbalance notion is that since the problem is a chemical one (supposedly), it requires a chemical (medication) to fix it. The logic here is that only chemicals can affect chemicals. Wrong again! What happens when you sneak up on someone and yell "Boo!!"? Their hair stands up, their hearts pound, they get a host of other unpleasant startle symptoms and they promise themselves to get you back. In other words, by completely non-chemical means, you have changed the amount of adrenalin in their bodies. No chemical was needed to affect their chemicals. What happens when you are terrified and having a panic attack in some enclosed place and you therefore leave. You calm down, right? So, if your panic attack was a chemical phenomenon, you have again changed it through entirely non-chemical means. Conclusion: it does <u>not</u> require a chemical to affect our body chemistry. Obviously. You can sit perfectly still in a chair and rev yourself up or calm yourself down just by what you think about. (We do it all the time – it's called watching TV.) So someone has told you that Panic is a chemical condition and therefore requires a chemical to change it? Give me a break!

Having gotten the Infamous Chemical Imbalance straight, let's consider which medications are available and what they can do:

# Anti-anxiety Medications ("Anxiolytics")

## Benzodiazepines

Pronounced "ben-zoe-die-**ay**-zeh-peens" if you are wondering. They are also called "benzo's" for short. This is a family of drugs that is familiar to most everybody even if you haven't heard that term for them. Common examples of these medications are Valium, Librium, Ativan, Xanax, Restoril, Halcion, Dalmane and Serax. (These are their brand names. Except for Librium, their generic names all end in "pam" such as diazepam (Valium), lorazepam (Ativan) and temazepam (Restoril).) If you've been treated at all for anxiety, you've probably tried at least one of these. If so, you have doubtless experienced their usual characteristics.

These are as follows:

They calm you down within about 30 min. to 2 hours. This depends upon which one you are taking and how sensitive you are. But they calm you down from Anticipatory Anxiety, not from a panic attack. For most people, taking a benzo during a panic attack does little more than make you feel really calm or sleepy **after the panic attack is over**. About the only exception to this if you go to an emergency room and get the benzo by injection and in a large enough dose to put an enraged logger to sleep. Literally.

Benzo's used to be prescribed just about like candy. They relieved stressed people and were believed to usually have no serious side effects. This medication La-La Land came to a crashing end with various suits for damages and the publication of books such as Barbara Gordon's "I'm Dancing As Fast As I Can", describing the nightmarish consequences of the authors' overuse of benzo's. In other words, it was discovered that they weren't so benign after all. For one thing, people who take them on a regular basis usually develop tolerance. This is the phenomenon of a drug losing its effect unless you take larger and larger doses. Just like habitual drinkers tolerate much more alcohol before getting the effect they want as compared with non-drinkers who feel ready to pass out after only two or three. The body has gotten used to the drug.

What usually goes hand-in-hand with tolerance is withdrawal. The body has made adjustments to compensate for the habitual presence of the drug. When the drug is not taken, the body that was ready to receive it is essentially "left hanging." This is drug withdrawal. And it does not feel good. In fact, many of the symptoms of withdrawal are the same as what you took these drugs for in the first place. Queasiness, anxiety and agitation are just a few. So if the drug has stopped working because of tolerance, you can't just quit taking the ineffective stuff or you will get the additional anxiety caused by withdrawal on top of your original anxiety! End result: you're worse off than you were to begin with.

If you've been through this lovely scenario, you know that the only way out is to slowly taper down off the benzo. That way, you get the withdrawal symptoms in smaller doses but for a longer time than if you just stopped taking it. And meanwhile, you have to handle your original anxiety in some other way.

In addition to these addictive qualities of benzo's, there are some further prices to pay for the good feelings they give. They interfere with memory and learning. One study showed twice the rate of motor vehicle accidents in older people who were taking them than in those who weren't. This was sharply illustrated for me one time when I was the passenger while my mother (who insisted that her doctor give her Valium) was driving. She turned from a side road onto a highway with one lane going in each direction. *But she turned into the oncoming lane!* I did not say anything at first, thinking that she would immediately correct the mistake. But she continued to blithely drive down the wrong side of the road without an inkling that anything was wrong until I finally had to tell her (or have a panic attack myself). For me, the most disturbing part of the incident was her telling me afterwards that she hadn't the slightest sensation of being drugged or affected by the Valium in any way! This impaired judgment as to your mental state means that you can't tell that you do not have your normal abilities. And if you don't know it, you won't take the steps necessary to compensate such as having someone else drive. This is certainly the most dangerous aspect of this kind of situation.

So do benzo's have any value for the person with panic? Yes. But not as medications to be taken regularly. They are fine when used once in a while – for instance to help you get through some particularly difficult situation. Like that visit from your sister with her spoiled kids and snobby husband. Taking an Ativan before they get to your house might be an excellent idea. It could really help you let it roll off your back when 3-year-old Dennis The Menace pees down your heating register. You can even take another Ativan a few hours later if the visit is dragging on. But do not let yourself find a reason to take one tomorrow.

Can't stop catastrophizing about that lunch date with the begonia club? Okay, cool out with a Valium that morning. It will last well through the afternoon and beyond. PTA meeting the next day? Uh uh. Save the Valium for then if you prefer, but do not take it two days in a row.

The same goes for using benzodiazepine sleeping meds like Dalmane, Restoril or Halcion. Occasional use in times of particular stress won't do you any harm (as long as you do not drive). But taking one each night will quickly stop helping while making it even harder to sleep than it was in the first place.

Incidentally, the main difference among these is how long they stay in your body. Dalmane (flurazepam) stays for days, Restoril (temazepam) for about one half to one day and Halcion (triazolam) for a few hours. I usually prefer temazepam because it will get most people through the night while not dragging on into the next day and beyond. I stay away from very short-acting benzo's like Halcion and Xanax (alprazolam) because they seem to let you down so quickly that you are having problems (and sometimes withdrawal) within hours of taking them.

The really best and most effective place for benzo's is in your purse or pocket. Seriously. The greatest benefit they confer is the knowledge that you have a way of lowering your anxiety if things get too rough. In my experience, they have done far more good for more people this way than they do by taking them. And you can see why:

Their pharmacological effect (what they do) is to reduce Anticipatory Anxiety. They do not halt an on-going panic attack. To say it another way, they reduce Catastrophic Thinking. Well, what does it do to say to yourself that things can't get too bad because you can always turn to this little bottle right here in your bag if needs be?... Right! You have just done some Cognitive Therapy (see Chapter 10) and reduced your Catastrophic Thinking. Putting it another way, you have just gotten the same result from knowing you have the benzo, that you would have gotten from taking it!!

So I do usually prescribe a benzo for most patients. And people do occasionally use them. But they mostly tell me that what's really important is knowing that they have it – for just in case.

[What you have just read is one instance of my differing from "mainstream" Psychiatry. The makers of some benzo's have placed groups of Panic Disorder patients on continuous daily use and have shown a decrease in panic attacks. (No surprise since they reduce Anticipatory Anxiety which causes most panic attacks.) They have thus obtained approval to advertise their drug as being indicated for the treatment of panic attacks. For the reasons above, I think this is a very poor way of going about treating panic attacks but it is an officially-legitimate treatment.]

## Buspirone (Buspar)

Buspar is in a class by itself. It is a non-benzodiazepine anti-anxiety agent. It does not have the associated tolerance and withdrawal of benzo's. Unfortunately, in my opinion at least, it also does not have their effectiveness. Unlike benzo's, it will not have an effect from taking a single dose. You must take it twice daily for at least a week for it to work. The proponents of Buspar claim that its gradual effect (unlike a benzo that you take and feel within 30 – 120 minutes) is what causes people to not really notice its effectiveness. They say that people who have not been spoiled by benzo's like it fine. Or, they say that the dose was too low. I say: "Would you guys like to come explain that to so many of my patients who have tried Buspar and return telling me that it doesn't work?" If it has been prescribed for you, it is worth giving it a try (assuming you are looking for an ongoing anti-anxiety medication). And if you <u>are</u> one of the people for whom it works, great.

## Antidepressants

Although benzo's do not prevent panic attacks except indirectly by decreasing Anticipatory Anxiety, there <u>are</u> medications that do. These are the antidepressants. They could equally well be called "anti-panics" but were first known for their effects on depression - hence their name. In my experience, they often don't cause panic attacks to cease altogether. But most antidepressants significantly reduce the number of panic attacks people have. Thus, they are the mainstay of medications prescribed for panic attacks.

There are many types of antidepressants. Some of the earliest were the Monoamine Oxidase Inhibitors (MAOI's) and the tricyclic antidepressants (TCA's). Both groups have many more side effects than the newer antidepressants such as Prozac and those that followed.

You can easily tell whether you have been prescribed a MAOI because there are dietary restrictions for people who take them. Namely, you cannot have fermented foods such as wines, cheeses and aged meats. Since no other antidepressants entail such restrictions, MAOI's are rarely used anymore. In the late 70's, the makers of these drugs sponsored much research to show that they are effective for panic attacks. In later years, the relevance of the research has been called into question. Nardil (phenelzine) and Parnate (tranylcypromine) are the main surviving members of this group.

Most people are familiar with one TCA or another. These include Elavil (amitriptyline), Tofranil (imipramine), Pamelor (nortriptyline), Norpramin (desipramine) and others. They are quite effective and remain in common use for a variety of conditions. Including panic attacks. They have in common a set of side effects that, in certain cases, can be quite hard to tolerate. These are dry mouth, temporarily blurred vision for fine print, constipation, difficulty urinating and sleepiness. Many other medications have these same side effects. If you are already taking one, adding a TCA may be just too much for you. On the other hand, one person may get a side effect quite strongly while another hardly experiences it at all. If you are one of the many people who can put up with the side effects, these may be great medications for you. (Always assuming that you want to go the medication route.) Especially because they are all available as generics and therefore cost very little.

Prozac (fluoxetine) ushered in a new era of antidepressants with great (but deserved) fanfare. The first group of these was known as "SSRI's" (Selective Serotonin Reuptake Inhibitors). In addition to Prozac, there are Zoloft (sertraline), Paxil (paroxetine), Luvox (fluvoxamine), Celexa (citalopram) and Lexapro (escitalopram). These have many fewer side effects while still possessing the virtue of preventing panic attacks. In fact, the only common side effects are indigestion if not taken with food and decreased sexual desire and performance (which can often be overcome).

The SSRI's are quite similar to each other. The main exception to this in my experience is that Paxil is often more sedating than the others. This makes it one of my first choices for Panic Disorder since it helps people sleep and, possibly, is calming throughout the day. Despite their similarity, if one SSRI does not work, another may still do the trick. So it is worthwhile trying a second or even a third.

Just yesterday, when I mentioned Prozac, yet another patient said that he had "heard bad things about it." This compels me to say that Prozac has long since been cleared of the charges leveled against it by an anti-medication cult shortly after it came out. It amazes me how the effects of their slur campaign live on more than 20 years later. (Eli Lilly Company: you can send the kickback now.)

Other antidepressants also prevent panic attacks. Some can show convincing research to support this. Cymbalta (duloxetine), Effexor (venlafaxine) and Serzone (nefazodone) are examples of this and you are not being used as a guinea pig if your doctor prescribes them for you.

**Anticonvulsants (Doesn't that sound terrible?)**
These are medications that were originally developed to control seizures. (No, as far as we know, panic attacks are not some kind of seizure.) In the early 90's, it was discovered that many of them are quite effective mood stabilizers as well. This means that they level out the highs and lows experienced by

people who have Bipolar Disorder (formerly called "Manic-Depressive Disorder"). In fact, they are often helpful for leveling out unstable moods from many causes. Don't get the idea that they make your mood flat – they just decrease the size of the swings.

These, too, have been tried for treating panic attacks. And there have been good results. Two of the better-studied ones are valproic acid (Depakote or Depakene) and gabapentin (Neurontin). Again, these are legitimate medications for your doctor to prescribe. Valproic acid blood levels are usually measured during treatment. Also, your doctor should keep an eye on how your liver, pancreas and clotting ability are doing. There is a strong warning against using it during pregnancy. Gabapentin appears to have a better side effect profile in general. At first this appeared to be a boon to people who had anxiety. Later research, however, has raised questions as to whether it is really effective. Antihistamines like hydroxyzine (Vistaril) are also given for anxiety but they may not be all that effective for you and have unpleasant side effects – namely, they dry you out and make you sleepy.

A number of other anticonvulsants are on the market. However, I would not be likely to prescribe them until there is more proof of their effectiveness.

**A Final Word** (about medications)

As previously mentioned, stay low and go slow. People with Panic Disorder are usually very sensitive to the effects and side effects of medications. Over and over, I have seen physicians prescribe a normal dose of an antidepressant only to have its side effects blow the patient out of the water. Unless you are willing to risk a really unpleasant experience, you should ask your doctor to start you on a very low dose and increase it very gradually. This often spells the difference between finding a medication and dose that suits you and never wanting to come near that awful stuff again.

Of course, this would have its upside, too. Because if you do not rely on medications, then you can turn more of your attention to what comes next – solutions that do not stop working if you stop taking a pill...

# Assignments for Chapter 8

## 1. Get out of the closet

As we noted in the very first chapter, people with Panic Disorder and Agoraphobia tend to be experts at concealing their conditions. This may save embarrassing explanations but it costs a lot more than it's worth.

To change something first takes accepting it. Hiding a problem is a great way of not accepting it. By hiding it, we are trying to create a false image of ourselves in the minds of other people. We do this because we think it looks better than the truth. So thinking the non-agoraphobic image is better than the agoraphobic truth, means that we aren't accepting the agoraphobic us as being okay. And trying to change what we criticize in ourselves just doesn't work. The criticism sets up a kind of resistance – as though someone inside us is saying, "I am too, okay. Even with my Agoraphobia." And you are.

So hiding the Agoraphobia and treating it as some dirty secret gets in the way of changing it.

I think this is why, at Alcoholics Anonymous meetings, each person who speaks starts by saying: "Hi. I'm Joe and I'm an alcoholic." Everybody responds: "Hi, Joe!" and Joe goes on to say whatever is on his mind.

Obviously, too, hiding the fact of your Panic Disorder creates a lot of anxiety over whether it will be discovered. This is just what you need to get over your panic – more anxiety (not!).

The only way to relax when you are walking on eggshells is to break every eggshell in sight. Then you can stop worrying about breaking one. So without further ado, here's the assignment:

Tell everyone you know that you have Panic Disorder! And explain to them what it means! (You: Oh, no! Me: Sorry – Oh, yes! This really is important.)

It does get easier after a few times. In fact, as you go on doing it (breaking the eggshells), you will begin to enjoy the resulting relief from your worry that someone will find out. Can you see what comes next? Yep. If you are not worried that someone will find out, you are beginning to feel like maybe you are an okay person even though you have Panic Disorder. (!!)

So, that's the assignment. You can see why you need to do it. So don't procrastinate. Make yourself a promise to tell one person a day until everyone knows whose finding out worries you.

## 2. Whole Body Relaxation

There are many relaxation methods out there. Here's one you will encounter under many different names that is tried and true:

You tense a set of muscles, hold them tense until you **really** want to let them go, take a deep breath in and then simultaneously let the breath all the way out, let the muscles go loose and say the word "relax." Easy.

Try it now with the muscles of your forearm. Rest your arm on a table, make a loose fist, bend the fist backwards towards your elbow hard, hold it until those forearm muscles are yelling for help, take a deep breath and all together: Let the breath out, release the forearm tension by moving your fist back to normal position and say the word "relax" as you do it. Doesn't that forearm feel good and relaxed?

Now, you simply do this with your entire body – muscle group by muscle group. You may wish to experiment with different ways of tensing each muscle group. Here are some suggestions that you can do sitting, standing or (best) lying down:

We will start at the feet and work our way up the entire body. Tense your feet by bending your toes under (hold, then breathe in and release breath and toes while saying "relax"). Tense your ankles and the muscles at the back of the calves by pulling your toes up towards your knees (hold, breathe in, release breath and feet while saying "relax"). Tense the muscles in the front of the calves by pointing the feet down like a ballet dancer (hold, breathe in, release and "relax"). Tense the thigh muscles by straightening your legs and attempting to bend your knees backwards (hold, breathe, relax). Squeeze the buttocks together (hold, breathe, relax). Suck your belly all the way in (hold, etc.). Extend the lower back by pushing your pelvis forward (hold, etc.). Tense the chest by pulling your shoulders back and squeezing your shoulder blades together. Tense your upper back by pushing your shoulders forward and towards each other. Tense your hands by clenching them into tight fists. Tense your forearms as described above. Tense your triceps by making your arms as straight as possible as though to bend your elbows the opposite way from normal. Tense your biceps in the approved "make a muscle" manner. Tense your neck by shrugging while bending your head back. Tense the muscles on the sides of your neck by bending your head first to one side and then to the other. (Each time still holding, breathing and relaxing.) Tense the muscles of your face by widening your eyes, raising your eyebrows, sticking out your tongue downwards as far as it will go and open your mouth wide. You can end by lying on your back with your arms extended above your head and your toes pointed down. Stretch your body to make it as long as possible. Then do a final hold, breathe in and let it all go while breathing out and saying, "relax" to your whole body.

Lastly, take an inventory of your entire body. Is there any tension remaining anywhere? If so, tense the appropriate muscle group, hold, breathe and release it again. Any tension anywhere else? No? Well, voila! You are relaxed!

Practice Whole Body Relaxation at least twice a day so that you build up your skill with it. You will need this for the next chapter.

## 3. Continue your Anxiety Diary and Chart

## 4. Continue your Field Trips

This week you might take a tour of 5 churches in your town. Maybe you'll see some beautiful art and architecture.

# CHAPTER NINE

---

## Habits And Behavior Therapy

## Or

## How To Unlearn Having Panic Attacks

---

Even though the cause of your panic attacks may have been removed by getting out of your traps, you might well have developed the habit of panic symptoms in response to certain situations. For example, your Life Trap has been resolved but you still have panic attacks when going to the grocery store. This is a habit. A habit is a physical response to a certain stimulus. Most people are aware of the famous example of Pavlov's dogs. Pavlov was a scientist who trained dogs to expect to eat after hearing a bell rung. He discovered that after a while, he could cause the dogs to salivate just by ringing the bell. They had developed a habit.

Habits can be undone in just the way they were created. The habit of developing panic symptoms when going to the grocery store was created by repeatedly doing that - going to the grocery store and having panic symptoms. To undo this habit, you need to simply go to the grocery store and not have panic symptoms. Repeatedly. This develops the habit of going to the grocery store without panic. This is Behavioral Therapy.

## Systematic Desensitization

Behavioral Therapists studied the process of forming and unforming habits. They came up with the most efficient ways to do this. One of the most important of these is called "Systematic Desensitization." This is a $10 word with a simple meaning:

When you go to the grocery store and get panic symptoms, you are said to be "sensitized" to going to the grocery store. When this being sensitized is undone, you are said to be "de-sensitized." When you go about desensitizing yourself in a systematic way, you are doing "Systematic Desensitization." But how can you be systematic about it?

Going to the grocery store has many parts to it: 1. You write out a grocery list; 2. You put on your coat; 3. You head for the door; 4. You go out to the car; 5. You drive down the street towards the grocery store; 6. You pull into the grocery store parking lot; 7. You get out of the car and start walking towards the store; 8. You go in the door; 9. You take a shopping cart and begin to walk around looking for the items on your list; and so on.

Each of these steps can produce anxiety symptoms. In other words, you can be sensitized to writing out the grocery list, or to putting on your coat, or to heading for the door. To systematically desensitize yourself, you take each of these steps in turn and develop the habit of feeling calm instead of anxious in response to that step. How to do this? Take the step and then calm down. You can calm yourself by any of the methods presented in this book such as Whole Body Relaxation, meditation or focusing. Let's say you have chosen Whole Body Relaxation as your method of calming down.

To systematically desensitize yourself, first go through enough steps to begin to feel anxious. Stop at that point and do your Whole Body Relaxation. When you are calm once more, start at the beginning and go through the steps to the point where you got anxious. Again, stop and do your Whole Body Relaxation. Go back to the beginning and do it all again. And again. Until you are not only calm when you get to that step but you are even bored. You can stop there for the day or you can go on.

To go on, start back at the beginning and go beyond that step until you again begin to get anxious. Do your Whole Body Relaxation and repeat the steps until you now can go all the way through this new step feeling only bored. Repeat this process all the way into the grocery store and through the checkout line.

Congratulations!! You have now systematically desensitized yourself to going to the grocery store.

Here's an example of how this works: You have decided to systematically desensitize yourself to going to the grocery store. So you write out your shopping list, checking whether you are beginning to feel anxious. No? Okay, so you put on your coat. Anxious yet? No. So you walk to the door, get in the car and back out to the street. Anxious now? Yes.

Okay. Drive back into the garage, walk back into the house, take off your coat and throw out your grocery list. Then practice Whole Body Relaxation until you are calm and comfortable. Next, you do it all again: write out a new list, put on your coat, go out to the car and back out to the street.

Anxious now? Yes, a bit. So it's back into the house, Whole Body Relaxation and try it again.

When you get out to the street the next time, let's suppose you are no longer anxious. What you do? Do you go on to the next step? No! Go back into the house and start all over again. The next time you get to the street, let's say you are still not anxious but are beginning to get bored with the process. Fine! Now it's time to move ahead.

You start at the beginning, get out to the street, find that you are still not anxious so you drive to the grocery store. Anxious yet? No. Fine. Then drive into the parking lot, park and get out of the car. Still not anxious yet? Okay, then go into the store. Anxious now? You bet!

Okay, fine. Get back in the car, drive home, do Whole Body Relaxation and start over with a new shopping list. Let's say that when you get into the store the next time, you are still anxious. So you repeat the whole process. Until you can do it all and be only bored with going into the grocery store.

But, you say, I still haven't done the shopping and I've spent hours slogging back and forth to the store. That's fine! Doing the shopping wasn't the purpose! You are spending the afternoon desensitizing yourself to going shopping. If getting the shopping done was the point, you could have sent someone to the store for you. Right? Although it may be tedious, what you are doing is earning yourself the freedom to go where you want. Not just for this time but for all the time.

Let's suppose that you have spent the afternoon at this and only gotten through the steps to get inside the grocery store. And now it's time for dinner. No problem. Your gains will remain. You have taught yourself to be able to comfortably enter the grocery store. You won't lose this. You can continue the process tomorrow. Perhaps it'll take one or two tries to get back to today's level of comfort, but not more. Then you can continue with the rest of your steps.

A study of Systematic Desensitization was done on people who had Obsessive-Compulsive Disorder. These people had a compulsion to do certain things such as repeatedly wash their hands. They washed whenever they shook hands with someone, touched another person, touched a doorknob and so on. They felt that they had to wash in order to avoid illness from getting other people's germs on them. In other words, these people essentially had a phobia of germs. (They felt just as embarrassed about this as you do about not being able to stay in a grocery store so no snickers please.)

Anyhow, they were given a Systematic Desensitization plan consisting of gradually exposing themselves to stimuli that made them anxious. Each time they became anxious, they would use a method such as Whole Body Relaxation to calm down before going on. So, for example, they would go to the library, open the door, handle books that others had touched, give the librarian their card to check out a book, etc. At whatever point they became anxious, they would use their relaxation techniques and then repeat the exercise from the beginning – *without washing their hands!*

The Systematic Desensitization was as effective as usual. People became more and more free to expose themselves to germs without becoming anxious and having to wash. No surprise - this result had already been proven. What the researchers wanted to study was whether the timing of the exposure made a difference. They found (and this is the point for your practice) that it did not matter what the timing was – only the total time of exposure to the anxiety-provoking stimulus. Thus, a person would get just as far by practicing Systematic Desensitization for 4 hours every other day for 2 weeks (28 total hours) as they would by doing 28 hours in 3 consecutive days or even by spreading them over two months. It is entirely up to you, therefore, how quickly you want to do the work of Systematic Desensitization and how quickly you want to reap the rewards. The more time you spend, the more you gain. Simple as that.

## Putting Systematic Desensitization To Work

You can work your way through all of your habits by using Systematic Desensitization. You have already (in Chapter 1) created your "Phobic Hierarchy." This is just a fancy term for a list of those things you have trouble doing. It is a hierarchy because you put it in order from easiest to hardest. Starting at the easier end, you can work your way through the list until you are free to do everything on it comfortably. This actually takes less time than you may think because you will be able to skip some items. For instance, you may find that once you have developed comfort going two miles from the house, you are also comfortable going 10 miles.

Here's an example:

A patient in Boston determined to become free to use the MTA. Whenever she got on it to go to work, she would panic. So, she bought herself a bag full of MTA tokens. And one Sunday, she got busy. She got on the MTA at the stop near her home. She went one stop away, became anxious and came back to the home stop. She relaxed herself and then got back on and went to the next stop again. And again until she was bored with it. Then she went two stops. And back. And two stops. And back again until she was bored with this. Next, she felt she could go four stops. She found there was still no discomfort so she went back to her starting point, got on again and went eight stops. At this point, she was beginning to feel anxious. So she went back to the start, calmed down and began again.

She conquered the MTA, then conquered going farther and ultimately tried her dream of crossing the country by train. Yep, a month later, she sent back a postcard from the West Coast. And she wrote her revelation of the first night: "I realized that wherever I was was home! From then on, it was easy!"

## Imaginal Systematic Desensitization

What if exposing yourself to even the first step of a stimulus causes you so much anxiety that you cannot get yourself to do it? Answer: use Imaginal Systematic Desensitization. This technique is the same as regular Systematic Desensitization except that you do the exposure in your imagination.

In this technique, you sit down in a quiet and comfortable place that is free from interruptions. You may want to close your eyes. Then imagine taking that first step in doing whatever you have chosen to work on. Make your imagining as realistic as possible. Add in the sights you would see, the sounds you would hear, what you would be physically feeling (temperature, wind on your face, etc.) and any smells or tastes. Imagine whom you would be with, what you would be wearing and what you would be doing (walking, sitting, carrying something, etc.).

To make it more realistic, you can ask yourself: "How do I know this isn't actually happening?" Whatever your answer, imagine that it is not that way. So, for example, if your answer is: "Because I can feel myself sitting in this chair", then imagine how it would be if you could not feel yourself sitting in the chair. Then, how do you know it isn't really happening? Suppose your next answer is: "Because I know that I can open my eyes and see the room I am sitting in." In that case, imagine that you couldn't open your eyes and see the room – it isn't there. Then how do you know it isn't really happening? And so on. This process helps you identify those factors that tell you that you are really not in the situation so that you can change what you are imagining to make it more realistic for yourself.

Once you have your imagined situation as realistic as you can make it, begin going through the experience of doing whatever you have chosen for desensitization. Just as in regular desensitization, as soon as you become anxious, stop going through the experience, come back to the room you are in and practice some form of relaxation.

After you have relaxed, go through the experience in your imagination again. Repeat going to the point at which you became anxious and then relaxing until you are bored with going through that part of the experience. Then, just as in regular desensitization, go on further through the experience until you again become anxious. Again, relax and desensitize yourself to this part of the experience. Continue on in this way until you can go through the entire experience with no anxiety. You have now imaginally desensitized yourself to the experience.

This imaginal desensitization will carry over to actually going through the experience in the real world. The more realistic you have made your imagined experience, the more comfortable you will be with the real experience. Sometimes, people make their imaginal desensitization so realistic that they completely desensitize themselves to the real-world situation. They then find that they can go all the way through the real experience with no anxiety.

This technique is especially useful for desensitizing to situations that are not available for practice such as airplane travel. An example in my practice occurred with a mechanic who had become phobic of reaching into automobile engines. This had come about when he had the experience one time of reaching way in and, in order to get at an inaccessible part, turning his hand in such a way that it became stuck. He could not get it out and no one was around to help. (Talk about a trap!) However he twisted, turned his hand, gently pulled, pushed or anything else he could think of to do, it would not come out. So he panicked. And in his panic, he just yanked his hand out, severely tearing it on various parts of the motor just to get it out no matter what. After this, he could no longer get himself to reach into an engine.

I took him through imaginal desensitization. He mentally approached a car, opened the hood, looked at the motor, touched something on the surface of it and became anxious. After he calmed down, we repeated this several times. When he was comfortable touching the surface, he mentally reached further and further into the motor – again stopping and doing relaxation whenever he became anxious. Ultimately, we got to the point of his hand getting stuck. After several tries (with stops to calm down), he could remain with his hand stuck in the engine without much anxiety. He then realized that it was his fear of not being able to get his hand out that had caused him to panic and rip his hand. It came home to him that if he had remained calm, as he now was, there <u>had</u> to be a way out since there had been a way in. It just took not panicking and slowly trying things over and over until he found it.

Mentally, he tried many ways of getting his hand out. We included imagining his getting frustrated and worried in the process. Finally, without any attempt on his part to make it happen, he found himself discovering the way his hand had gotten in the motor and it coming loose again. After this, he was able to mentally go through the whole experience in comfort.

It must have been quite a vivid experience for him because it completely carried over to real life. He was able to go right back to working on automobile engines without needing any further desensitization. Also, the entire exercise took him about two hours. This was certainly a small price to pay for getting his vocation back.

## Exposure or Flooding

No, this isn't about going around in a storm with nothing under your raincoat. It's about facing what you fear. And it's probably the single most powerful technique for overcoming panic attacks there is. A very wise man once said that a fear not faced becomes the center of your life. If you are an agoraphobic or have panic, you don't need that explained.

So, you have to face (expose yourself to) what you fear. You can do this gradually as in Systematic Desensitization. Or, you can do it all at once. This is "flooding." You simply flood yourself with what you fear. Nope, you won't go crazy or explode into little bits. And unless you are in a quite precarious heart condition already, you won't have a heart attack. Believe it or not, what happens is that after a while, your heart slows down, your breathing becomes regular and your whole body normalizes. Fact.

One of the pioneers of Agoraphobia treatment, Dr. Manual Zane of The White Plains Hospital phobia program, has an audiotape called "I Never Stayed In The Dark Long Enough." Although his talk is not about flooding, it does make the point that if you stay with what you fear long enough, you get over your fear of it.

Flooding is simply doing this all at once. The human organism just seems to be built in such a way that it cannot sustain fear of a particular stimulus indefinitely. In fact, it cannot sustain it very long at all! That is why I am very skeptical when someone tells me she has panic attacks that go on for days. We just cannot keep up such a level of physical and mental arousal for that long. Even people who think they have panic attacks for hours usually do not. When they keep an Anxiety Diary, rating how much anxiety they experience, they usually find out that their anxiety fluctuated during those hours. They (rarely) may have worked and reworked themselves into a series of panic attacks. But a single panic attack almost never keeps going like that. Check it out for yourself.

People have long realized that exposure to fears reduces those fears. And avoidance increases them. That's the reason for the old saying that you should get right back on the horse that threw you. And it's also why you should quickly return to any new place where you have had a panic attack. Do not let that place be added to your avoidance pattern. That's how avoidance patterns grow.

This is not for everyone - maybe it is not even for most people. But if you are really gutsy or determined to kick this thing right now, it can be done. Use flooding. Just go into that supermarket and stay there until you are no longer panicking. Period. That's it. And it works. And will keep on working.

Tough? You bet. Effective? You bet, again.

# Assignments for Chapter 9 (and from here on):

## 1. Start Using Systematic Desensitization

You have already constructed your Phobic Hierarchy in Chapter 1. Begin chopping away at it using Systematic Desensitization. Use Imaginal Desensitization first for difficult steps.

## 2. Try Flooding

You can do a mild version by flooding with a stimulus that does not have very high levels of anxiety associated with it.

## 3. Practice Whole Body Relaxation

If you are using it during your Systematic Desensitization, you are already practicing it.

## 4. Out of the Closet

Continue telling people that you have Panic Disorder. If anyone important to you still does not know it, tell them.

## 5. Charts and Trips

Your Anxiety Diary and Chart as well as your Field Trips can now become a part of your Systematic Desensitization.

# CHAPTER TEN

## Cognitive Therapy

### Or

### "As a man thinketh in his heart, so is he."

Proverbs 23:7

Anything that can cause an outpouring of adrenalin will give you a pounding heart, rapid breathing, rubbery knees, butterflies in the stomach and all the rest of it. And lots of things cause an outpouring of adrenalin: 1. Falling in love and seeing your loved one crossing the room towards you. 2. Becoming angry. 3. Watching an exciting movie or sports event. 4. Even laughing hard.

As you begin to consider this, you will likely find there are times when you really do not know whether you are feeling fear or anger or love or amusement. After all, any injection into your system of adrenalin will cause all the panic symptoms. And what is your usual response to feeling your heart pounding, your breathing becoming rapid and shallow, butterflies in your stomach and rubbery knees? You probably conclude that something terrible is happening. But, for example, unless you have correctly divined that your boyfriend is actually an axe-murderer in disguise, what is really going on may be love.

The point to notice is that your physical feelings give rise to certain thoughts. And these thoughts may be correct (e.g. "I love him.") or incorrect (e.g. "I'm about to die.")

The reverse is also true: what you think can cause your physical sensations. Obviously. Just remember the old horror movie scenario that goes like this: It's a dark, foggy night. The light of the single, dim street lamp casts a human-like shadow on the wall. It is holding what appears to be some blunt object by its side. It grows larger and larger while steps are heard approaching. The camera flashes on the terrified face of the heroine. The shadow has meanwhile become enormous. She opens her mouth to scream. But then the person causing the shadow walks into the circle of light. It is a small child carrying a teddy bear by one leg. And we give a great sigh of relief. Moral: what we thought caused what we felt.

So the principle is:

**Thoughts and feelings can cause bodily responses and bodily responses can cause thoughts and feelings.**

Furthermore, it's really easy to get into a vicious cycle with this. You have the thought: "I do not think I can go to the women's drumming group tonight because I might have a panic attack." Next, you check out your feelings to see if that feels correct. And sure enough, you can picture it being hot and noisy and you can already feel some twinges of knots in your stomach. Noticing these, you think to yourself: "Yup, I'm already feeling anxious just thinking about it. In fact, it's beginning to feel like I'm going to have a panic attack right now." Next, you check out this thought by focusing more on your body to see if your heart is beginning to feel funny, too. And thinking about that feeling, you begin to feel it as well. So this gives you the thought: "Oh God, here it comes!" And the thought gives you more panic feelings. And the feelings give you more thoughts. And away you go.

So what's a poor girl (or guy) to do? Cognitive Therapy to the rescue!!

Cognitive Therapy has repeatedly been proven highly effective for Panic Disorder as well as for a host of other conditions. It is based upon the principle that your thoughts control your feelings. So by changing your thoughts, you can change your feelings. And what's the main kind of problematic thinking in Panic? You know it by now - **Catastrophic Thinking!!**

So Cognitive Therapy for Panic and Agoraphobia works largely by undoing Catastrophic Thinking. And there are lots of ways to do this:

## Thought Stopping

One of the simplest and earliest techniques of Cognitive Therapy was called "Thought Stopping." And it means just what it says.

First, pay attention to your thoughts. As soon as you catch yourself doing some Catastrophic Thinking, stop it. The main way to stop thinking about something is to think about something else. One commonly used alternative thought is created by visualizing a red, octagonal Stop sign like you see on the road and, in your mind, yell the word: "STOP!!" If you are alone, you could even yell out loud. Simple though this is, if you diligently do it for a couple of days, you will find that you quickly develop the habit of replacing your Catastrophic Thinking with the "Stop" visualization/ verbalization. And guess what happens in your body when you stop your Catastrophic Thinking?

## Focusing

Another thought replacing technique is called "focusing." In this technique, you first pay attention to your thoughts. As soon as you catch yourself doing Catastrophic Thinking, you focus your attention on something else. Anything else. Planning what you'd like to do on your next vacation is fine. Picking out a name for your son's coming baby would be good. Trying to remember your mother's recipe for that great cheesecake would work. Anything on which you can plant your thoughts will do the trick.

This works well with feelings, too. In fact, it is one of my favorite techniques to use *during a panic attack.*

Okay, your heart's pounding, you feel short of breath, you think you are going to pass out and so on. Now tell me how many ceiling tiles there are in each row. No, you do not have to pay attention to your breathing. That won't help anything. And it's <u>not</u> more important than the number of ceiling tiles. In fact, the number of ceiling tiles is the single most important thing in your life, right now. COUNT THEM!! OUT LOUD!! NOW!!

Focusing on repetitive sensations in the immediate environment seems to be especially helpful. Also, engaging more than one of the five senses is useful – especially touch. Feeling the texture of the seat of the chair on which you are sitting or the pressure of the chair against your back are two examples. Counting is another good focus. So counting the number of different types of surfaces you can touch from where you are standing is often done. Or counting red cars per mile as you go down the road. And so on.

I recall going through the tunnel to the airport in Boston as a field trip with a couple of agoraphobics. The traffic through the tunnel was slow and one person panicked. I steered with my left hand and held hers with my right. Together, we pounded our held hands against the seat, focusing on counting how many times we could hit it between each of the lights on the tunnel wall. Bang – one thousand one. Bang – one thousand two. Bang – one thousand three. And so on until we reached the next light and started counting from one again. This also had the virtue of measuring the number of seconds it took to get from one light to another so we got some feeling of making progress while we were at it.

And here's the ultimate focusing method: Focus on one of your panic symptoms and *try to make it worse!* Yep, your eyes do not deceive you. And I know this seems like the last thing in the world you would want to do. But it is actually the most powerful thing you can do during a panic attack, amazing as it seems. If you've never done this, you will be surprised at what happens - the symptom gets better!

For example, you've been busy trying to get your heart to slow down. And I'm telling you to try to speed it up. Scary thought, huh? But you will find that you not only can't speed it up by focusing on it and trying to will it to go faster. Instead, it'll slow down. Same thing with any panic symptom that is not under voluntary control. (Breathing is under voluntary control and, of course, you can breathe faster if you try.) But this works with trying to make your knees more rubbery, collecting more butterflies in your stomach and even sweating more.

There are two things to remember when doing this. First, we are talking about trying to directly make the symptom increase. Not indirectly. By now, we all know that you can indirectly make any symptom worse. That's what Catastrophic Thinking was invented for. Want to make your heart go faster? Easy. Do not focus directly on your heart. Instead, think about what everyone will say when you have a panic attack and faint at Aunt Victoria's family reunion next month. Your heart will respond quite well. And you can run the rate up even more by worrying that you are having a heart attack right now.

So that's not the technique. The technique is paying attention directly to how your heart is feeling now as it pounds away and trying to mentally push it to pound more.

The second thing to remember when doing this is to focus - do not jump around. If you are working with the knots in your stomach, stick with trying to make them more knotted. Do not go from your stomach, to your heart, to feeling dizzy, back to your stomach, to feeling sweaty and so on. That's another technique for freaking yourself out which you have already perfected. It does not need more practice.

## Cognitive Mistakes

More recent Cognitive Therapy (see the works of David D. Burns, M.D. in Recommended Reading) has focused on what can be called "Cognitive Mistakes." These are errors in thinking. Everybody makes them. One example is Black-and-White thinking. Perfectionists do this a lot. For example, if you weren't the life of the party, you conclude that you have the social charm of a slug. Or, if the job isn't perfect, then to the perfectionist, it's a mess. (By the way, Cheri Huber makes the point that so-called perfectionists are really "imperfectionists" since they are so focused on the 5% that's imperfect instead of the 95% that's fine. Good point, no?)

You can see that the conclusions being drawn by the Black-and-White thinker are just plain untrue. They are mistakes. And they can sometimes be quite serious mistakes. For example, deciding that one is a social write-off could and has resulted in people never meeting or dating others, never getting married, never having a family and sentencing themselves to lives of loneliness and regret.

Another Cognitive Mistake is called "Overgeneralization." This is a great one for creating agoraphobic avoidance patterns. It consists of mistakenly concluding that because something has occurred in one or two instances, it will occur in all instances. (Can you guess where this is going?) Because you had one or two panic attacks in the supermarket, you have mistakenly concluded that you will always have panic attacks in the supermarket. The actual fact may be that you had the panic attacks because of some trap going on in your life at that time which is already resolved. But your overgeneralization not only causes you to avoid supermarkets, but it is also a self-fulfilling prophecy. Namely, your expectation of a panic attack at the supermarket creates lots of Anticipatory Anxiety when you try to go there. Your expectation therefore escalates your anxiety the closer you get to the store. And by the time you enter the door, voila! Your conclusion was right – you have a panic attack. (Q.E.D. – Quite Easily Done.)

So that ancient person who wrote Proverbs was right – the way you <u>think</u> it will be for you is the way it <u>will</u> be for you. James Allen, who lived from1864 to 1912, wrote an interesting little book on this point with the title: "As A Man Thinketh." It remains so inspiring to people that they have placed the whole book on the Internet for free. He is quoted as saying: "All that a man achieves and all that he fails to achieve is the direct result of his own thoughts." And this gives us a way out because we can change our thinking. That is the essence of Cognitive Therapy – identifying Cognitive Mistakes and correcting them.

What do you do? Simple:

Pay attention to what you are thinking.

Identify the Cognitive Mistake (mistaken thought).

1.  Correct it.

Our self-proclaimed social cripple could solve her problem by repeatedly: 1. Noticing that she is taking the fact that she was not the most popular person at the party to mean that she is completely socially unattractive, 2. Remembering: "Aha. This is Black-and-White thinking" and 3. Telling herself something like: "Just because I'm not the most popular person does not mean I'm not likeable at all. Actually, there were lots of people at the party who were much less a part of things than I was. And I don't feel that they had no right to be there so why should I feel that I can't go to parties? Actually, there was that kinda cute guy who looked lost and didn't talk to hardly anybody. Maybe if I see him again, I'll just ask someone to introduce us..."

What to do about Overgeneralization?

Pay attention to what you are thinking.

Identify the Cognitive Mistake.

1. Correct it.

In the case of the supermarket Overgeneralization, the process would go like this: You have made the kids' sandwiches and notice that you are almost out of peanut butter. You instantly think: "Oh, no. Not a trip to the supermarket." But you just read this chapter last night. So you remind yourself: "Aha. Here's the very problem I just read about. Now, what was the deal about it? Oh, yeah – I'm supposed to pick out the mistake in my thinking and correct it. Yeah – I'm Overgeneralizing from having had trouble with the supermarket before. And the correct way of thinking would be that just because I had trouble there before does not mean that I will have trouble there now."

So armed with the thoughts that this is a new day, that you have made many changes since you last had trouble at the supermarket, that you have your Emergency Kit with you (See Chapter 3) and that this can be an opportunity to practice Systematic Desensitization (See Chapter 9), you: (This is a quiz. Pick one.)

A. Send your husband out for peanut butter.

B. Tell the kids that jam-only sandwiches are just as good.

C. Decide to spend some time today working towards your own freedom. And if you save yourself asking your husband to get the peanut butter, all the better. If not, you are still better off because however much of the shopping trip you desensitize yourself to will last until you next work on it.

**Other Cognitive Mistakes** (again see Dr. David Burns)

Dwelling In The Dark: You pick out the negative aspect of a situation and pay attention only to it until everything seems to be negative.

Feeling Out Reality: Taking what you feel as an accurate indication of what is going on. We already discussed this regarding your axe-murderer boyfriend: You had the same feelings you would have if he were an axe-murderer, so he must be one. Makes sense, right?

Rejecting The Light: Like Dwelling In The Dark, you ignore anything positive. Instead, you say, "it doesn't count." For example, you dispose of the times you went to a movie and enjoyed yourself by saying that they do not count and you will certainly have a panic attack if you go tonight.

Being Psychic: Knowing things by magic. For example, you know that others are thinking badly of you even though there have been no words or actions to even hint that this is the case. Thus, you could only know that people are looking down at you by means of your psychic abilities such as reading their minds. Predicting negative events in the future with no material or rational basis for your foreknowledge is another psychic ability. You should hang out your "Fortuneteller Is In" sign.

Exaggeration: When both good things and bad things happen, you exaggerate the size of the bad things and minimize the size of the good.

Giving or Taking Blame: You hold yourself responsible for occurrences that were only partly under your control if at all. Or, you give out responsibility to someone else who only had a partial say in the matter. For example, thinking that you wrecked everyone's picnic because you did not want to go even though *they* chose not to go without you.

## Hidden Beliefs

Why do we make such silly errors in thinking? Are we crazy, irrational beings? No. The answer is that we are blinded to what makes good, rational sense by our underlying beliefs.

For example, why exaggerate the bad things and minimize the good? Because we are unconsciously fitting reality to our beliefs about it. Sherlock Holmes repeatedly corrected Dr. Watson for inventing theories as to who committed the crime and then trying to bend and twist all the facts to fit them. In the same way, if we have a hidden belief that "Life is a never-ending series of problems", we automatically focus on the events that confirm our belief and sort of do not even see the events that contradict it. This may make us unhappy, but it achieves something more important to us: we are on solid ground – life is predictable. You know that old saying that we would prefer ten devils that we know to one that we do not? Same thing. We know how the ten devils are going to torment us. But that is preferable to an unknown torment by the stranger devil.

So even though our beliefs (by means of our Cognitive Mistakes) keep us in an unhappy world, it is <u>our</u> unhappy world. The one we know and know how to live with.

Each time you note a Cognitive Mistake in your thinking, you get a clue as to the hidden belief that underlies it. By asking yourself: "Now why did I distort things that way?", the belief behind the mistake soon emerges. For example: "Now why did I take all the blame for everybody not going on the picnic?" "And why did I exaggerate the effect of my not making a bigger party for my daughter's birthday?" " And why did I predict that everyone would dislike it when my mother came to help out while I was sick?" Soon, it gets pretty hard to miss what all these misapprehensions have in common: the belief that you always ruin everybody's good time.

As you identify your Cognitive Mistakes, keep an eye out for the beliefs that fuel them. Learn what kind of world you are keeping going by means of misperceiving what is really going on. After all, the familiarity is really not worth it. One devil will never torment you as much as ten.

# Assignments for Chapter 10

## 1. Thought Stopping

For one week, practice Thought Stopping every time you begin Catastrophic Thinking. You will know when you are engaging in Catastrophic Thinking because you will find yourself feeling anxious about some event that is coming up.

## 2. Focusing

Practice focusing 10 minutes daily for at least a week. Alternately focus your attention on what you hear, see and touch. Learn what absorbs your attention the most easily and completely. Remember: you are developing a skill to use during a panic attack so you have to become _really_ good at it. Try focusing your attention on bodily sensations like your pulse. Try to make it speed up. Don't worry. See what happens.

## 3. Cognitive Mistakes

Write out a list of the Cognitive Mistakes. Carry it with you together with a pen and notebook. Try to identify at least 5 examples of Cognitive Mistakes daily. (There are many more going on all the time.) Look for the common factors in your Cognitive Mistakes so you can identify the underlying beliefs. Begin to put together a picture of yourself and your world according to your hidden beliefs. Write it down.

## 4. Phobic Hierarchy

Continue working through your Phobic Hierarchy using Systematic Desensitization. Continuing your Anxiety Diary, Anxiety Chart and Field Trips be can part of this.

# CHAPTER ELEVEN

## Insight-oriented Therapy: Part I

## Or

## Why??

When I was in med school, I asked my Psychiatry professor, which, of all the different schools of psychiatric practice, he thought was best. He replied that in his opinion, psychodynamic psychiatry was the most complete explanation of human feelings and behavior the West has to offer. I have found that he was right.

So, what is it? Psychodynamic psychiatry is the knowledge of human psychology that started with Freud and has been developed and added to for most of the 20th Century and ever since.

I think Freud's greatest contribution to Western culture was his asking the question: "Why?" Specifically, "Why do people act and feel as they do?"

Big deal, you say? Well, actually, it is a big deal. Because when he asked the question "Why?" he made a crucial although obvious assumption – the assumption that there was an answer. In other words, he somehow dreamt up the idea that human feelings and behavior had reasons behind them – that there was some kind of logic to them – a psycho-logic. This is such a vital and basic idea that nowadays, we just take it for granted. We talk in terms of being in denial or projecting feelings onto each other or suppressing our anger or having low self-esteem or being traumatized. We have no doubt whatsoever that there are reasons for our suffering. Can you imagine a time when people had little or no idea that there were reasons (*internal* reasons) behind what they went through? They must have felt like they were living in a whole different world.

Freud's purpose in identifying what went on behind the scenes was to find out what was causing things to go wrong so they could be set right. It also turned out that just by understanding why we feel as we do often makes the correction obvious or even automatic. One small example of this is the "anniversary reaction":

Ever had a day when everything was just going wrong? And even the things that were going right somehow were all wrong, too? You just seemed to have gotten up on the wrong side of the bed? Well, you could have been having an anniversary reaction. And if you were, you'd instantly know that that was the problem if someone reminded you that this was the day someone you cared about died. You would know it because the moment this fact came to your attention, everything would change. You'd feel sad and perhaps miss the person, but your irritability and sense that all was not right with the world would vanish.

Perhaps you have experienced this. If not, the next time you are feeling all out of sorts, ask yourself if today is the anniversary of a loss. If it is, you will be surprised at how just the conscious realization of that fact causes everything to change. And that is the point: becoming consciously aware of what's going on under the surface can automatically change things.

This brings us to the definition of the word "insight." "Insight" means becoming consciously aware of what's going on inside yourself. So insight-oriented therapy works just that way - it produces change by providing insight.

Perhaps you've already experienced this by reading about traps. You might have said: "Hey – that's what's going on with me." If so, you had some insight. And the change in your life resulting from this insight follows right along automatically - without your having to do anything. For example, you might have realized that you need to say "no" to something you've been making yourself go along with. If so, you will soon experience how this realization changes what you feel and do.

Usually, insight-oriented therapy takes place in a therapist's office. (If you decide you need this help, see Chapter 7 on selecting a therapist.) But insight occurs by your looking within yourself. And there's only one person required for that. So it is also quite possible for you to get your own insight - if you know where to look.

So here's where to look:

## Anxiety Chart and Diary

First, you need to become aware of what you are actually dealing with. This is why you have been diligently keeping your Anxiety Diary and Anxiety Chart. If you have been writing down what caused your anxiety to go up, you have made a good start on figuring out the "why" of it. By reviewing them periodically, the Anxiety Chart and Diary will begin to reveal what the various times you became more anxious had in common. You have probably already done this to some extent. Instead of simply knowing that you get more anxious in the supermarket, dental offices, church, movies and airplanes, you have probably realized what all of these situations have in common – that you cannot leave them without calling attention to yourself or making an embarrassing scene. See if you can find the common denominator among other situations that increased your anxiety.

## Identify your traps

Just like that, huh? Well, 'yes' for some people and 'no' for others. But even if it's the biggest thing you've ever taken on, it's got to be done. So gird your loins and let's go for it. If you decide that now is not the time for you to get out of your overall "Life Trap", that's okay. It will still help you in major ways to identify it.

Many people know what is the overall trap going on in their lives without any effort. Just this week as I am writing this, a brand new patient asked: "So why does this happen?" I'm sure she did not expect a real answer because she certainly looked surprised when I gave her one. I told her about traps.

And as I described how people go into periods of having more panic attacks or fewer panic attacks depending upon whether they are in traps in their lives, she just kept nodding and saying stuff like: "Uh huh. Uh huh. That's right. I <u>see</u> that!" It was at the end of the appointment, so I have to wait until next week to hear what her traps actually are. But it was clear that she knows.

So if you know what your Life Trap is, you can skip ahead to "How To Get Out Of Your Trap" in the next chapter. If not, read on.

A lot of what an insight-oriented therapy seeks to show you is where to look to find the answers you are seeking. Here's a pointer for where and how to look for your Life Trap:

It's a phrase I just can't resist putting in: "Subsequence often implies Consequence." These are $10 words saying that something that happens <u>after</u> something else (subsequently) is often <u>because</u> of it (a consequence). For instance: you got sick to your stomach <u>after</u> going out to eat so you conclude that it must have been <u>because</u> (a consequence) of something you ate. Subsequence implies consequence. Cool, huh? (Not the sick stomach, however.)

Yes, it's relevant. An excellent question to ask in order to identify your Life Trap is: "What did the panic attacks start after"? And an excellent way to figure this out is to do a Life Chart. In fact, this is very worthwhile even if you do know what your trap is.

## Your Life Chart

This approach, as applied to Bipolar Disorder, was first employed by Robert Post, M.D. On the page after next is a sample Life Chart. It roughly shows the frequency and intensity of panic attacks by the height of the boxes and it shows the ages at which they occurred. There are notations as to major events going on in this person's life at these ages. Can you discover the common factor among the various periods during which she had panic attacks - what they happened after? Skip ahead, study the chart now and think about it before you read the answer.

Here is what the chart shows: From 5 to 6 years old, she had a number of panic attacks related to starting school (a common occurrence in pre-agoraphobic children). From 15 to 19 years old, the panic attacks came back fairly severely and frequently. This period was kicked off by her father's death. At age 24, they came back with similar severity when her first husband began drinking. This continued until age 28 when her doctor gave her Paxil to take. This cut the panic attacks approximately in half until she was 36. At that time, she quit the Paxil and there followed 2 years of even worse panic attacks than before she started it. At 38, she got divorced and the panic attacks tapered off to the level they had been when her husband started the drinking. At age 41, she met and later married Sam. The panic attacks stopped altogether. However, when she was 44, Sam was diagnosed with an enlarged prostate and the panic attacks returned with moderate severity.

Have you figured out the common factor? The (all too common) answer is... loss. Our subject first got panic attacks (in itself a very good clue) when having to start school – i.e., loss of home and parents each day. Then she got them again when her father died. Her husband's drinking was like not having the guy she married anymore. And Sam's prostate condition now threatens the loss of him.

By the way, this does not mean that she is doomed to always have panic attacks because life always has its losses. Her problem is not that there are losses but that these represent a (guess what?) trap for her. For reasons such as having learned that she must always be "the strong one" who never cries or falls apart, she does not allow herself to grieve her losses. This means that she is stuck with some very strong feelings and no outlet for them. So what happens? Panic attacks, of course. But there is a way out. She needs to grieve. How can she get help with this? See for yourself: Type the words "Grief Group" in the "Search" box on the Internet computer at the library or in your home. See what happens

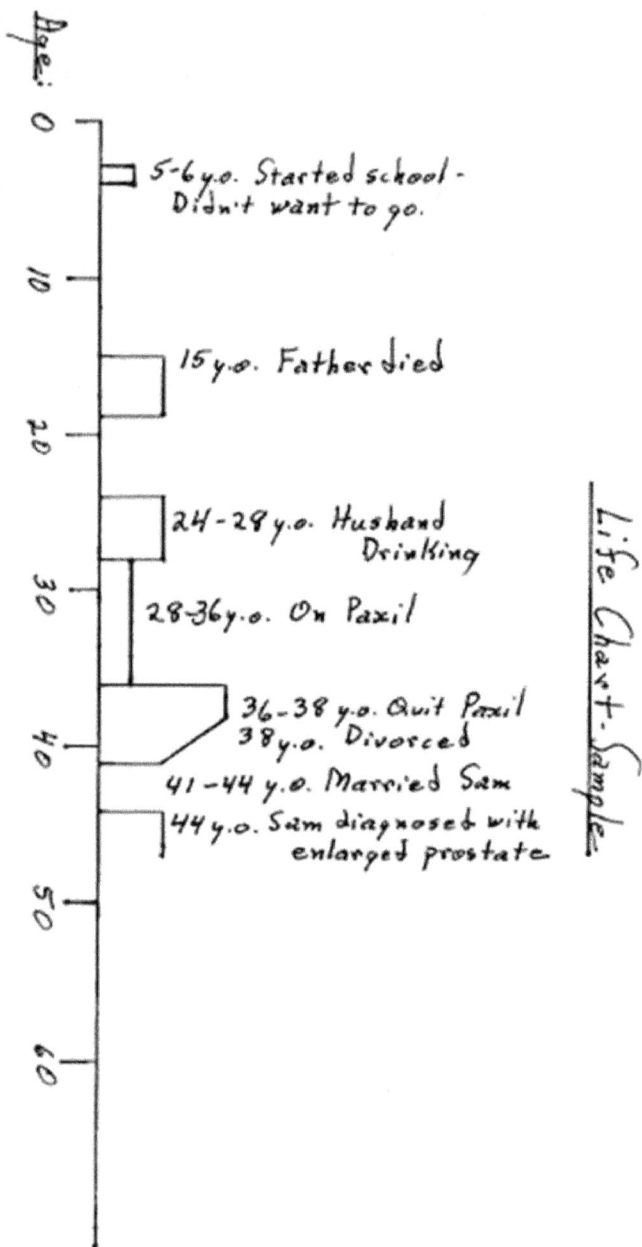

Age:

0

5-6 y.o. Started school - Didn't want to go.

10

15 y.o. Father died

20

24-28 y.o. Husband Drinking

30

28-36 y.o. On Paxil

36-38 y.o. Quit Paxil
38 y.o. Divorced

40

41-44 y.o. Married Sam

44 y.o. Sam diagnosed with enlarged prostate

50

60

Life Chart - Sample

## Here's another example:

When Ken was 6, his father died in an accident at work. His two sisters are 14 and 16. He was the product of an unplanned pregnancy. With his father gone, the family has too little money to get by. His mother just can't manage raising the kids and working as well. She decides to accept her sister's offer to care for one of the children. She picks Ken for this since the girls will be out on their own in a few years anyhow. Not surprisingly, Ken had his first of a series of panic attacks the day he is supposed to go live at his aunt's house.

The panic attacks eventually tapered off until an incident in high school: The tough boys hung around together. They taunted smaller boys like Ken – calling him names like "fag." When he tried to hit one of them, several boys grabbed him and held him helpless while they pulled off his pants. He ran after them but some girls saw him running in his underpants and laughed at him. Ken finally made it to the boys' room. His next series of panic attacks began then and there.

Ken's next spate of panic attacks started with his being laid off from work. The company was doing poorly and someone had to go. They picked on Ken even though he had more seniority than some of the other workers because they had to keep up their quotas of minority employees. At this time, Ken had undertaken an expensive series of orthodontic treatments for his little daughter. If he did not have the job, he did not have the dental insurance to cover the treatments. What could he do? Jobs weren't easy to get. He couldn't just have the dentist pull the braces off her teeth. They were already partly straightened. If only it weren't for those quotas. It just wasn't fair. He resumed having panic attacks.

Here's a one-question quiz:

Ken is a person who is likely to develop a panic attack if:

a) His daughter was the only kid to forget her lines in the Christmas pageant and the other parents teased him about it afterwards.

b) His wife told him she wanted a divorce because she just did not love him any more.

c) His auto insurance was unfairly raised after an accident that was the fault of the other person but who lied about what happened and was believed.

The answer is… whatever would make Ken feel unfairly and helplessly angry. That is the common denominator in the situations that brought on panic attacks before – being picked as the kid to lose his home, being bullied because he was smaller than the other kids and being laid off because he wasn't a minority. So, in the quiz, the third choice would certainly do it. The others could do it also if you imagined them as making Ken feel helpless anger. Thus, if he felt angry because there was something unfair that caused his daughter to forget her lines (like the lines were changed at the last minute), the first choice could give him a panic attack. The second one also could if there was something about his wife wanting a divorce that made him feel helplessly angry. An example would be if she wanted a divorce because she had turned to someone else as a result of Ken being away from home a lot, working.

On the other hand, if Ken just felt embarrassed about his daughter forgetting her lines or just hurt and rejected by his wife wanting a divorce, these situations would not result in panic attacks.

Ken would do well to draw up a life chart showing his periods of panic attacks and what situations had preceded each period. He could then look for the common denominator that was present in each situation. When he finds the correct one, he'll quickly know it because it will apply to the little, daily situations as well as to the large events of his life.

For example, we have figured out that the common denominator for Ken is anger – especially anger over something that was unfairly done to him and which he is helpless to do anything about.

So, just as we did with our quiz, we can predict the situations that will cause him to panic. We know that if Ken is the thirtieth car stuck while the drawbridge is going up, he probably won't have a panic attack. But if they let a long line of cars through and pick on Ken as the first car to stop to wait for the bridge, we've got a pretty good guess that he's in for trouble.

Here's a list of frequent common denominators. As you go over the significant events in your life chart, if your common denominator does not leap out at you, try asking yourself if it is one of these:

- Sadness

- Grief

- Anger

- Frustration

- Embarrassment

- Humiliation

- Fear of Death

- Fear of Injury

- Fear of Loss

- Fear of Failure

- Longing To Be Loved

- Helplessness

- Being Smothered

- Being Abandoned

- Feeling Overwhelmed with Responsibilities

- Not Having Control

- Addiction

In fact, all suffering can be boiled down to:

1. Being without someone or something you want to be with; or

2. Being with someone or something you want to be without.

So, another approach to figuring out your Life Trap is to ask yourself: "Who or what am I with that I want to be without; or who or what am I without that I want to be with?" As you look over the list above, everything on it is included in this question. Thus, we can be without people we love, we can be without security, we can be without power to do something, we can be without health or success. Also, we can be with people we dislike, we can be with too many responsibilities and we can be with the knowledge that we made fools.

Remember, too, that traps involve I-Can't-But-I-Must double binds. So you could also ask yourself: "What do I feel I must do but can't?" Again, the answer will be your trap. If you ask: "What do I feel I must do in my life but can't?" the answer will be your current Life Trap. If you ask: "What do I feel I must do today but can't?" the answer will be your immediate, Day-to-Day Trap. This trap could be the same one as your Life Trap, or it might be a smaller version of your Life Trap. Ken getting stuck as the first car made to wait for the bridge would be an example of a small version Day-to-Day Trap.

If you have done all this and asked yourself all these questions and still can't figure out what your Life Trap is, you could ask someone who truly cares about you. Tell them not to hold anything back because you really need to know: "In what way do you see me as being trapped in my life?" Especially if you explain why you are asking, the two of you should be able to come up with it. (Unless your friend is rolling on the floor with laughter that you could seriously ask something so obvious.)

Finally, the last resort:

---

You've made a life chart and no pattern of subsequence and consequence is visible. You've gone through the list of possible common factors among trapping situations and none of them seem to apply to you. You've asked yourself who or what you are without and want to be with and vice versa. You feel you've got everything you strongly want. You consider the ICBIM double bind and feel that you can do everything that you must without undue stress. And your friends and loved ones agree that there is no major problem in your life or how you are taking things. You are really stuck – no traps.

What this means is that your unconscious mind is hiding something from you. And from the people who know you as well. (Yep, it can do that.) So, at this point, you need the assistance of someone who is trained in unearthing what goes on in people unconsciously – namely, a therapist. An insight-oriented therapist.

When you go to a therapist, you can make it clear where you are coming from – that you are not looking for a prolonged revamping of your character. Instead, you can explain that you are looking to understand how you are trapped in your life because you are working your way out of Panic Disorder and need to know this. So (you explain), what you are after is a good, thorough evaluation to be followed by a frank and open discussion of the therapist's conclusions. You should ask if the therapist is agreeable to this. Because you do <u>not</u> want a long therapy that attempts to gradually bring you to those same conclusions yourself. And you do <u>not</u> want the therapist to hold things back to spare your feelings. You are paying for the straight scoop and want to know that that's what you will get. If the therapist is not agreeable to this, then you will need to look further for one who will give you what you are paying for.

Such an evaluation should only take a few hours – I'd say six at the very outside including giving you the results. You can also ask for the therapist's written report of the evaluation. There should always be one.

# Assignments for Chapter 11

## 1. Life Charting

Make a Life Chart and identify the Life Traps that caused the periods of increased panic attacks. Also, find the common factor behind these Life Traps (like Ken's above).

## 2. Life Trap

Identify your current Life Trap.

## 3. Field Trips

Continue going on Field Trips. You might take a drive in the country where you do not normally go. Or visit a lake or the seashore.

## 4. Charts

Continue the Anxiety Diary and Anxiety Chart. Review them for common factors in your Day-To-Day traps.

## 5. Hidden Beliefs

Continue your Hidden Belief list (Chapter 10).

# CHAPTER TWELVE

## Insight-oriented Therapy: Part II

### Or

### How To Get Out Of Traps

(Answer: Just do it.)

Sorry, but no kidding. You can think and analyze and therapize and go to psychics or astrologers or do aromatherapy or practice Feng Shui or do crystals or nutritional supplements or get on Prozac or, or, or... but, in the end, you just have to bite the bullet and leave your trap.

I know – you say that if you could have gotten out, you would have done so already and you wouldn't be trapped. Right? Well, remember our definition of a trap? It was: "Any situation we do not want to be in but from which we can see no acceptable way of escape." In other words, we can see no way out *without paying a price we do not want to pay.*

So there's always a way out – in fact, there are usually more than one. But we are trapped because we have decided that the drawbacks of each way out are too great to be worth it. For example:

Remember our little league mom? She was trapped because if she did not enslave herself to supporting the little league team, then she would be judged and looked down upon by the other little league parents. (And her own conscience, of course.)

So there <u>was</u> a way out of her trap. She just regarded the price of getting out as unacceptably high.

Another example: Remember Sylvia? The price of getting out of her trap of being married to an abusive husband certainly was quite high. She had to face the fear of what he threatened to do if she were to leave him. She had to find a way to support herself and her baby and maybe find that she wasn't able to. If she left, she had no place to go and might be homeless. And so on. She is stuck - because the price of leaving is too high.

But is it? In fact, Sylvia's situation is all too familiar to therapists. They call it The Battered Wife Syndrome. They know the fears that keep the wife in the abusive relationship. And they know what has to happen (and usually does) for it to end.

What's that? The battered wife has to reach the end of her tolerance for the relationship. She has to "bottom out" in alcoholism parlance. This means that she has to reach the point that she is so fed up with the abuse that she would rather face up to all her fears of leaving than go through one more day of it. So, fears or not, she goes.

Although you could never convince her of it beforehand, the price of leaving the trap usually turns out to be far less than she had imagined. There are "Safe Houses" which solve the problem of where to go, how to feed the baby and herself for the short-term and how to be safe from retaliation by Darrell if he really even wants to carry out his threat. There are social services that provide money for longer-term food and low-income housing. There are agencies to help her get a job and daycare for the baby while she is working or going to school. And so on. She just had to be ready to take the plunge.

However, until she is ready, there is really nothing anyone can do. Time and again, therapists tell their battered wife clients about the ways out. And time and again, the clients tell the therapists all the reasons why they are trapped and can't leave. So the therapists just shake their heads and say to themselves: "Some day she'll have had enough."

So the answer to the trap is another of those simple-but-not-easy things. In this case, it is – just leave the trap. Often, it is quite hard. No one is pretending that it's not. But when you have bottomed out with life in the trap, you will do it – come hell or high water.

## Bottoming Out

When I was in residency training, I was assigned for six months to be the doctor for an alcohol detox ward at Boston State Hospital. The ward covered South Boston, which was pretty famous for the amount of alcoholism going on there at the time. While working on this ward, some of the patients explained to me the concept of "bottoming out." I have found it to be applicable to all sorts of human problems:

The guys told me that an alcoholic would not quit drinking until he had "bottomed out." Bottoming out was simply reaching the point that the cost of drinking was just too much to go on doing it. Something went off inside – some decision made itself – and the alcoholic "just knew" he'd had it with drinking. It was no longer an option.

They also told me that alcoholics had high, middle or low bottoms. A "high bottom" drinker reached the point of quitting when he had lost his wife, kids, his job and his home – and found himself sitting in freezing doorways drinking cheap alcohol out of a bottle in a paper bag. (You see these guys in doorways in every city.)

A "middle bottom" drinker bottomed out only after he'd lost all these things but also had been brought to emergency rooms more than once, vomiting blood. He was bleeding into his esophagus so severely that if they hadn't been able to give him transfusions in time, he would have bled to death. The ER doctor usually had told him that the next time would be his last. They just wouldn't be able to sew up the burst veins in his esophagus one more time. That experience might bring the middle bottom guy to the end of drinking.

And the "low bottom" drinker did not reach his bottom this side of the grave.

I also learned from these guys that until someone reached his bottom, nothing was going to get him to stop drinking. It did not matter how convincing you were or how good his intentions. If he hadn't bottomed out – if that switch inside him hadn't been flipped, he was going to keep drinking. I think this is why Alcoholics Anonymous has a central concept of "a Higher Power however you understand it." We do not have the power to flip that switch. It seems to be built in. If losing wife, kids, etc. is enough for us, that's just the way we're built. If it isn't – again, that's how we're built.

So on the detox ward we learned to be honest and unblaming with each other about the bottoms. If a guy hadn't reached his bottom yet, it was okay: He was going to go back to drinking and that's just the way things were. Nobody ragged on him about it. And nobody tried to get him to rag on himself. He was going to drink and we'd see him and help him dry out the next time he came through the detox ward. And hopefully, there would be that next time.

I learned from the guys that the best help I could be for someone was to give him the facts of his case straight with no sugar coating and accept him wherever he was in the process. We didn't need to pretend with each other. We understood what it would take to quit drinking and if that hadn't happened yet, then so be it.

We help each other and we help ourselves the best if we accept ourselves as we are - honestly and without judgment. Without whipping ourselves into changing. Instead, simply learning the facts about our situations and having compassion for ourselves if we can't yet get unstuck.

So I'm going to give you the straight facts about remaining in traps. If you can't get out yet, that's okay. But it may help you reach your bottom to know what those panic attacks mean and what those traps cost you.

## Back to Panic

In the end, most traps are ways that you are not being true to yourself. It is not being true to yourself to keep subjecting yourself to physical or emotional abuse like Sylvia was. It is not being true to yourself to sacrifice your life to the wants of your baseball-playing son as our little league mom did. It is not being true to yourself to live a life of many "shoulds" and very few "wants." It is not being true to yourself to rarely have fun. It is not being true to yourself to live in fear – of regret or loss or guilt or shame or physical harm. Joel S. Goldsmith, a 20th century mystic wrote a book entitled: "Man Was Not Born To Cry" (see References). So true. On many levels.

Panic attacks can quite literally be considered as representing messages from an inner part of you. The messages you are being sent are something like: "Look out! Danger! If you do this thing, you will be losing part of your life!!" Because to spend time not being true to yourself is to not really be living during that time in your life. And those hours are gone forever from the hours you are given to be here on Earth. Is it any wonder that the physical and emotional response to life robbing situations is the same as the "fight or flight" response that animals have to life threatening danger?

What happens if you ignore the message? Well, what happens each time an animal is in danger? Sure. It gets the same "fight or flight" response. So ignoring the message just causes it to keep being sent. In fact, as people spend more time being untrue to themselves, the intensity of the message increases. It's as though an inner self is yelling louder and louder to get your attention. This is why you will have panic attacks as long as you stay in your trap. And they may even increase in frequency or intensity. The tension of not being true to yourself can build and build until something must give – you get a panic attack.

Here, we arrive at a strange point that is always reached in the overcoming of Panic and Agoraphobia: the realization that **the panic attacks are actually your friend!!** They are warning you that your life is going away without being lived. And they are pushing you to learn this and get your life back.

Sometimes, it looks to others that the agoraphobic is just being selfish by using the fear of a panic attack as an excuse for not doing something she does not want to do. You also may have thought this about yourself. If so, you did not understand that you would not be feeling a panic attack was in the offing if your life weren't already overly weighted in the direction of doing "shoulds" rather than "wants." In other words, your insides knew that another trip to the grocery store was going to be that extra straw that would be just too much. It would be just that extra bit that was too much of not being true to yourself.

When all is said and done, you simply must get out of your Life Trap if you want to overcome your panic attacks. Medications can cover it up temporarily, but that inner you will still be sending its message somehow. It is my belief that if you take away its ability to express the message through panic attacks, it will find some other way – like physical illness. Something is telling you that you are not living in a healthy way for you. If you are willing to heed that inner something's message, your only choice is to get out of your trap.

Remember Audrey who was trapped in the Rehab Hospital at her mother's side? I suppose she could have taken medications and gone on living there. But this was not her way of dealing with problems. She had entered a costly treatment program for Agoraphobia. It was getting nowhere. No amount of persuasion, education about Panic Disorder or encouragement succeeded in moving her out of the nursing home. Finally, the therapists had to give her the choice: either get out of the hospital or take a full refund of her money and quit the therapy. Because, they explained, she would only be wasting everyone's time and effort if she hoped to stop having panic attacks while remaining in her trap.

Audrey came close to accepting her money back. But, in the end, she made the choice to be true to herself rather than to submit herself to her fear of guilt over her mother. She went home. The panic attacks stopped.

There could have been a call one day that something awful had happened to her mother. Audrey had had to decide that even though this was possible, she had to live her own life and be part of her family. She knew that she had provided as well as she possibly could for her mother's needs and that she had to let it go just as a parent cannot follow her child to school every day to make sure no bully picks on him. It wasn't easy. But Audrey knew it was right. And, as so often happens, the consequences of breaking out of her trap were not the disaster she had imagined. She could have gotten that call from the nursing home. But she never did.

## Your Life Trap Inventory

Here's an exercise in self-honesty that really takes courage: Take a piece of paper and draw a line down the center of it. At the top, write out the name you give to your trap. For example, "Dating A Married Man." Label one column "Pros" and the other "Cons." Then, honestly and ignoring all your judgments about each item, write out everything you get from staying in the trap and everything you give up. It does not matter what each entry makes you look like. Be ruthless. If it's true, put it down.

Here's an example for Sylvia's trap:

## Life Trap: Leaving Darrell.

### Pros

- I'd stop getting hurt

- He's not really here

- He's not happy either

- I'd stop having panic attacks

- I'd stop having my life go by while I stay where I'm unhappy

- Etc.

## Cons

- I do not believe in divorce

- My child needs a father

- I will lose my home

- I won't have any money

- I'm afraid to be on my own

- I love him

- He'd hurt me if I left

- He'd get someone else and I'd be out in the cold where I'd deserve to be

- Nobody would want me, especially with a baby

- It's too hard to raise a child on your own

- A divorcee is a loser

- Mother will say she told me so

- Etc.

The point here is not weighing pros and cons or seeing which list is longer. The point is being honest with yourself and getting it all down. Doing it in your head, you may bounce from one pro to one con and back to the same pro and then to another con and so on until you've just got a headache. This way, if you have any further thoughts, you can add them to the inventory *and then just move on.*

Any decision you discover will not be a matter of weighing things in your mind. It will be the result of reaching your bottom about your trap. Getting all the issues down in black and white will free you up to do whatever is right for you at that time instead of just spinning your mental wheels. It may be right to give yourself permission to stay in your trap for the time being. Or it may be right to move on.

My brother has an excellent method of resolving indecision: He flips a coin. Then, if he finds he's really unhappy about how it came up, he knows that he wants to do the other thing. All we are after here is clarity about the issues involved and where you are about them. Remember: getting things out into the light of conscious awareness often results in their getting healed without your having to do anything else.

I am extremely grateful that a long time ago, the realization came to me that **decisions aren't made, they are discovered.** Weighing pros and cons and then making a decision doesn't work. We don't have the ability to <u>make</u> a decision. And if we do something based upon a made-up decision, we will be forever looking over our shoulders because the issue really is still undecided. Decisions happen inside of us by themselves –

such as the bottoming out decision. All <u>we</u> can do is to discover a decision that has already been made. Meditation is a great way to do this. And such discovered decisions are always the right ones – we never regret them.

Overall, then, the way to get out of your Life Trap is simply to be honest with yourself about what staying there is costing you and let your heart do the rest. You will know when you've bottomed out and are ready to make the change. (It could even be now.)

# Assignments for Chapter 12

## 1. Bottoming Out

Write down 5 examples of bottoming out experiences of yours or someone you know.

## 2. Being Untrue To Yourself

Write down all the ways you are not being true to yourself.

## 3. Being True To Yourself

Write down all the ways you are being true to yourself.

## 4. Inventory

Do a Life Trap Inventory for your Life Trap.

## 5. Charting

Continue the Anxiety Diary and Chart.

## 6. Field Trips

Keep the momentum of your Field Trips going. Can you find a free trial dance lesson?

# CHAPTER THIRTEEN

---

## Meditation

## Or

## How To Become Relaxed and Aware

---

### Why Meditate?

Meditation is a valuable method of self-growth that adds to Behavioral, Cognitive and Insight-oriented therapies. In recent years, it has become increasingly recognized that meditation greatly helps our bodies, our minds and our emotional states. A few decades ago, it was considered to be some strange and useless practice mostly engaged in by gurus and people wearing saffron-colored robes who chanted in the street. I can recall my parents referring to it as "contemplating your navel." As Western scientists have studied it, they found that meditation produces some very real and tangible benefits.

---

Blood pressure and heart rate go down to healthier levels. Abnormal heart rhythms like atrial fibrillation become normal. Physical and emotional tension are reduced thereby putting less strain on the heart, causing less acid secretion in the stomach, decreasing headaches, increasing immunity to illness and more. It seems that just about everything in our bodies works better when we are relaxed.

The same is true for our minds and emotions. We perform better at mental tasks when we are not tense. We concentrate better, think faster, are more creative and remember more. Emotionally, too, we are much improved. When relaxed, we are happier, more loving, more forgiving, less frustrated and more able to laugh.

Although meditation is a great way to get in a relaxed and healthier state, that was not its original purpose. Instead, meditation has accurately been called "awareness practice." This is because it consists of practicing being aware of all that is going on in our here-and-now experience.

Most of the time, we allow our attention to flit from one thing to another without even being conscious of where it is directed. This is kind of like being in a dark room and shining a flashlight here and there but without even paying attention to what we are lighting up. Thus, we decide what to have for lunch, think about whether we came off okay when telling our friend about our latest worry, we feel angry at the jerk who just pulled his car out in front of us, we recall that crash we read about where two people died, we think how the news has nothing but gruesome stuff to report, we consider limiting the amount of TV the kids are watching and on and on. But if someone offered us 50 bucks to tell her everything we had thought for the last five minutes, she would probably be able to keep her money. It's like our eyes saw the stuff in that dark room but our minds were somewhere else.

Now if we went into that dark room with some good incentive to come out able to report what was in there – like we'd get $5 for each item we could name – we'd do a lot better. This is the essence of meditation – paying attention to what we are aware of each moment. Not just being aware of it, but being conscious of the fact that we are aware of it. So we wouldn't just think about how we came off to our friend, we'd <u>pay attention to the fact</u> that we were thinking about how we came off to our friend. In other words, we might say something to ourselves such as: "Oh, now I'm re-running my conversation with my friend to see how I came off." <u>Then</u> if someone were to ask what we'd been thinking about, we wouldn't get splinters from all that head scratching.

Someone jokingly described a meditation teacher asking a student what she was aware of during her meditation. She responded that she had heard a bird singing outside. "Yes," said the meditation teacher, "but did you hear the bird while breathing in or breathing out?"

So meditation is practicing being conscious of what we are aware of. It not only has the physical and emotional benefits mentioned above, but we learn how to live consciously rather than going around kind of dreaming all the time but having forgotten the dream as soon as we try to recall what we were dreaming about.

## How To Meditate

(Sorry, but it's another of those SBNE things. You know - Simple But Not Easy.)

There are all sorts of styles of meditation depending upon what philosophy or religion your teacher espouses. Here is a simple, non-denominational and generic set of meditation instructions. They contain all the essentials for obtaining the benefits we are after:

1. Sit in a comfortable chair with your feet flat on the floor and your hands resting in your lap. Unlike meditation practices requiring uncomfortable body postures like the

lotus position, our goal is to make your body comfortable so that you can forget about it as much as possible. Do whatever works for you. Most people find that sitting upright in a non-reclining chair that is not too soft remains the most comfortable throughout the meditation period. You are welcome to sit against the back of the chair.

2. Before you start, choose a focus. Your focus is something on which you will steadily keep your attention throughout the time of your meditation. The reason for having one is that it is much easier to become aware of what your attention has strayed to if you have been keeping it on a particular focus than if you have just been freely floating around in the silence. More on this in #5.

The rise and fall of your abdomen as you breathe is one of the more common choices of focus. Some people prefer to repeat a word with each breath such as "peace" or "relax." Others prefer a short phrase. Still others prefer to focus their attention on some other spot in the body. The area just above the bridge of your nose or the sensation of the air going in and out of your nostrils are examples.

You should experiment with different foci until you find one that fits you well. Then stick with it unless you really feel that you must switch to something else. Definitely do not change foci during a meditation. Decide beforehand what it's going to be and stay with it during that meditation period.

3. Set a timer or some sort of alarm for the length of time you have chosen to meditate.

4. Close your eyes and let your attention rest on your focus.

5. Your mind will inevitably stray to thoughts (like "this is stupid"), feelings (like your nose itching), planning (like what you are going to do as soon as you are through with this), sounds (like people talking in the next room), wonderings (like wondering if you are doing it right) and so on. Now comes the essence of meditation: *try to be aware of whenever your attention has strayed and gently bring it back to your focus.* Your goal is NOT to never stray from your focus – this is impossible. Instead, your goal is to become aware of what you are paying attention to as soon as you can and then bring your attention back to your focus.

You will quickly understand the term used amongst meditators – "monkey mind." The mind jumps from this to that to that just like a monkey jumping from branch to branch in a tree. Your mission (and you should choose to accept it) is to keep track of where the monkey is.

One author (Stephen Levine, see Recommended Reading) likens the meditator to a person sitting on a hillside overlooking a railroad track. As an endless train goes by, you observe what is in each car, trying to never get caught up in what is going on in any one of them. Instead, you notice what is in the first car as it goes by and then shift your attention to the second as it goes by. There may be things of great interest in some of the cars but you move your gaze to the next one anyway. So, one car may contain a man eating breakfast, the next a vision of paradise, the next a child playing, the next a bomb exploding, the next a couple making love, the next a person looking embarrassed and the next a scene from your vacation at the beach. Of course, while meditating, each time you notice that you are looking at some scene in a railway car, you turn your attention back to your focus. You stay with your focus until you become aware that you are looking in another railway car. Then (guess what?), you go back to your focus. I don't imagine you will be shocked to learn that a number of the cars contain a bored person (you). But you may be surprised to find that if you note the bored feelings and go back to your focus, they go their way after a few times just like all the other scenes in the cars.

6.  Your alarm goes off and your meditation is over.

## Some Additional Tips

If it can be said that there is any goal to what you do in meditation, that goal would have to be awareness of where your attention is at each moment. In other words, go back to your focus after each of the railway cars. For example, if your focus was your breathing, it might go something like this: "Oh, now I'm watching a child – back to breathing – Oh, now I'm seeing a bomb explode – back to breathing – Oh, now I'm watching them make love – back to breathing…etc." This, of course, is the unreachable ideal. But it is the direction your efforts should take in meditation.

One direction your effort should <u>not</u> take is going with your judgments about how well you are doing. It is natural to have those judgments but they are no truer or more worthy of your attention than anything else you see in one of the cars. In other words, they should be treated as: "Oh, now I'm making a judgment about how badly I'm doing – back to breathing…"

Although it takes effort to be constantly catching yourself when you go off thinking about something other than your focus, there is a corresponding sense of relaxation afterwards. It seems as though the more effort at being aware you make, the more relaxed you feel later. (Yes, it's a strange sort of exercise that leaves you more energized the harder you work but it does.)

At first, your meditation periods can be 10 or 15 minutes once or twice a day. You can gradually work up to 30 minutes twice a day, which is ideal. There is no such thing as too much meditation. The more you do, the healthier it is for you. Little periods of meditation throughout the day are also very useful. Meditation "centers" you. This means that it brings you back from whatever you have gotten caught up in to a calm place from which you can see things in perspective.

Example: You are in the middle of making dinner and you get a call that one of the kids has "used the 'f-word'" to his teacher and is being held in the principal's office until you get there. 5 or 10 minutes of meditation before you go is an excellent way of getting back to the "big picture." Nobody is injured or bleeding. The house hasn't fallen down in an earthquake. Nobody will starve to death if dinner has to be late. If you do not kill that so-and-so kid yourself, there's every reason to expect that he'll reach his next birthday. So take that 5 or 10 minutes to sit down and pay attention to your breathing. The world won't end and you will doubtless handle everything better for having gotten centered.

Meditation is also the best way of relaxing as part of your Behavior Therapy (See Chapter 9). Each time you go further in your Systematic Desensitization, you will need to relax and bring your anxiety level down. You can use Whole Body Relaxation as described in Chapter 8 or you can use brief meditations for this. Since the more you meditate, the more powerful it gets, it soon becomes a highly effective way of reducing anxiety.

Most importantly, meditation is the primary means of increasing your awareness. All day long, you are bombarded with events, thoughts, feelings and reactions. Allowing what goes on inside to pass by unnoticed is to be living in that dream world which mostly evaporates the moment you try to recall it. What did you do, think and feel yesterday? It's mostly gone. A week ago? Blank. The you who lived then is forgotten. She did not register then so you surely can't get her back now.

Meditation changes that. You develop your awareness of what you are conscious of – and so your experience does not pass by unnoticed. And the habit of being aware carries over from your meditation periods to the rest of your life. You are more present all day long. So you do not store up unnoticed angers, disappointments and tensions. You increasingly notice them as they occur and, just like the bomb that explodes in the railway car, you let them go and pass on to the next scene that comes. This prevents such emotions and reactions from hanging around in your unconscious mind creating anxiety or physical illnesses like ulcers and headaches.

Early on, I found that my patients who had psychologically-caused physical illnesses denied having any emotional problems. They would say: "This <u>can't</u> be psychological. I feel fine!" Well, of course they felt fine. They had neatly disposed of their feelings by converting them into physical reactions – like secreting more stomach acid. If they <u>felt</u> their emotions rather than turning them into physical responses, they wouldn't have to be eating milk toast and wondering how they could have burned holes in their stomach linings. In fact, such people have been found to not even have the words in their vocabularies for many of the emotions. A fancy word has been coined to denote this –"alexithymia" (literally, "without feeling words"). Persons who develop psychologically-caused physical illnesses are commonly found to be alexithymic. They are so unaware of their feelings that they have never even developed the vocabulary with which to express them.

The point is that *it's the unconscious stuff that gets you*. Conscious anger will never eat a hole in your stomach. Only anger of which you are unaware will do this. And the essence of meditation is developing your ability to be aware. (Remember - "awareness practice"?). So, of course it improves your health.

Finally, meditation is the loving thing to do for yourself. You are paying attention to you. And you are taking time out to get back your perspective. It does not matter if the TV is blaring and traffic is roaring by. Just go into your room, close the door and start paying attention to whatever you are aware of. If it is the noise outside the room, fine! Just notice it and go on to the next railway car. It has been said that you should be able to meditate at a football game. Of course! Does your awareness shut off at a football game? So you can pay attention to what you are aware of at the football game. And you may also find that there is a silence going on behind all sound. (Hmm...)

# Assignments for Chapter 13

## 1. Meditate

Begin meditating, of course. Start with 10 minutes twice a day. It does not matter a bit if you find that your mind has wandered for most of the meditation time. Some days it wanders more, some days less. What matters, and matters greatly, is that you sit there for the time you have allotted to meditation being as aware as you can of the passing train. Just do it. Who knows? Maybe someone will issue you a beautiful saffron-colored robe.

## 2. Continue Anxiety Diary, Anxiety Chart and Field Trips

Is there a meditation group nearby that you can try out? Meditating with others often is very different and sometimes it is much better.

## 3. Traps

Keep adding to your "Traps" Diary.

# CHAPTER FOURTEEN

---

## Field Trips

## Or

## Getting Out In The World

---

One of the many benefits of meditation is that you are practicing being aware of your experience rather than just being mindlessly in your experience. This means that you get less and less caught up in what is going on. Instead, you become more able to watch what is going on and see it from a new vantage point. You will, for instance, become aware of how silly it is that we insist upon certain ways of doing things and judge anyone who does them differently as "crazy." We all spend a lot of time trying to make sure no one sees us as crazy. Fear of this judgment fuels much of peoples' Catastrophic Thinking about going somewhere and having a

---

panic attack. ("What will everyone think if I have to run out of the supermarket, leaving a full shopping cart behind?")

On the other hand, do we really <u>know</u> what everyone will think if we run out of the supermarket. Not to mention – do really we care? In one of our treatment programs, a therapist always used to give a demonstration of this point. The therapists and patients would all go to a local restaurant, order some food and, midway through the meal, this therapist would stand up and fall to the floor as if she had fainted. Did everything stop? Did sirens go off and the police come rushing in? Did other diners move away in horror?

The results would invariably be laughable. Mostly, people just ignored her and continued eating. There would be one or two offers of help and that was about it. Think of all the time that all those patients had catastrophized: "What if I go to a restaurant, have a panic attack and <u>faint</u> right in the middle of everything!?" All that good catastrophizing for nothing!

You might say that being ignored could be expected in a big city. But it wasn't a big city. It was a small, wealthy, upper middle class suburb. Also, I must admit that the first time she did it, I rather cringed at what I imagined the people around us were thinking. But that, of course, was the whole point: What if they did think we were weird? Were we concerned that they would reject us if we invited them over for tea? Would word of this get back to the IRS and we would be put in a higher tax bracket? It's amazing how conditioned we are. I had even known it was coming, but still I felt somewhat embarrassed!

So that's the point: there is no substitute for experience out in the real world. In this chapter, you will first be armed with instructions for dealing with Anticipatory Anxiety or a panic attack. Before going out into the world, read them over carefully. Imagine yourself in a situation where you will need to use them. Imagine yourself using them. <u>Fully</u> imagine that. If any useful additions occur to you, put them on the copy of the instructions you will take with you.

The most important principle to remember if you experience Anticipatory Anxiety or a panic attack is that these are opportunities to learn. No kidding – ***these are opportunities to learn!*** Do not let them go by unused. The goal is not survival. You will survive no matter what. You already checked this out with your doctor. The goal is to make use of what happens. Do not let yourself end up just having had an unpleasant experience. That would miss the whole point. Make sure you end up having gained something from the experience.

You do this by observing the experience as it occurs. The reason for having a notebook and pen in your Emergency Kit is to write down your observations. If you write them down, they will not just flit into your awareness and be instantly forgotten in the stress of the moment. If you are practicing meditation (as per Chapter 13), you will be strengthening your ability to observe. This will aid you in these situations. Copy these instructions and put them in your Emergency Kit. You will practice using them in the next assignment.

# Instructions and Reminders In Case of Anticipatory Anxiety

(Write the responses to all questions in your notebook.)

1. Remember: You can always bail out when you choose.

2. You can bail out by:

   - Leave the situation causing the anxiety, or

   - Take a benzodiazepine and wait 20 minutes.

3. In your Anxiety Diary, note:

   - The time when you first noticed the Anticipatory Anxiety.

   - The level of the anxiety.

   - What you are anticipating that makes you anxious.

4. Every 10 minutes, note the time and the level of your anxiety. (Set an alarm for 10 minutes later each time you have noted these.)

Write down: Is the anxiety telling you something useful such as that you are getting into a trap, or is it based on a Cognitive Mistake? (You may need to consult the list of Cognitive Mistakes.)

If the anxiety is telling you that what you are getting into is not being true to yourself:

- Write down what it is and why it is not being true to yourself.

- Correct the error. (E.g. "I'm sorry, but I realize that I really do not want to...")

- Continue to track your anxiety every 10 minutes until it is gone.

- Use relaxation techniques if necessary.

5. If the anxiety is due to a Cognitive Mistake, continue as follows:

6. Write down which Cognitive Mistake is causing the anxiety.

7. Write down why this is an example of that Cognitive Mistake.

8. Write down the undistorted fact of the matter.

9. Write down any belief involved in the distortion.

Write down a behavioral plan to desensitize yourself.

10. Relax yourself using Meditation or Whole Body Relaxation.

11. Begin your behavioral plan whenever you like.

Continue to track your anxiety level in your diary.

**Example:**

Apr. 4, 2011 - 5:10 P.M.: Lisa came home to announce that she got a part in the school play on June 17. Anxiety: 5.

Cognitive Mistake - Overgeneralization. Reason it's a mistake: I'm not uncomfortable every time I go to a school function. Unmistaken fact - I could really enjoy it. Belief - I'm not as good as other parents. Desensitization Plan: Attend rehearsals weekly until I really feel comfortable about going to the performance.

5:20 P.M. - Anxiety - 4. Will meditate.

5:40 P.M. - Anxiety - 2. Somewhat looking forward to trying out my plan. Will start on Fri.

# Instructions and Reminders In Case of A Panic Attack

1. Remember: You can always bail out by exiting the situation even if it is embarrassing to do so.

2. Remember: You have had many panic attacks before. They feel terrible. You always survive them.

3. Remember: You always end up being okay sooner or later. The time this one will have lasted is already going by.

4. Remember: Panic Attacks are usually over in 20 – 30 minutes, often leaving you calmer than before.

5. Remember: This is an opportunity to learn vitally important facts about your panic attacks. Do not waste it!

6. Remember: Do not fight it! Your mind and body will automatically return to normal no matter what you do right or wrong.

7. Write down the time it started and what triggered it.

Write down the time and the severity of each of your symptoms every 5 minutes.

8. Write down what you are believing about it, e.g. that it will kill you, that you will go crazy, that you will faint, that you have to make it stop, etc.

9. Count your heartbeats for one minute and write down the result.

10. Try to make your heart go faster for 3 minutes.

11. Again count your heartbeats for one minute and write down the result.

12. If it got faster, repeat #11 and #12 until it slows.

13. Count something in your environment – like pleats in a curtain or tiles on the floor.

14. Are you still having the same beliefs about the panic attack after 10 minutes? Write down your answer.

15. Meditate for 5 minutes. Write down what happens.

16. Pace back and forth. Write down what happens.

17. Compose a letter to me telling me why I'm all wet.

18. If you are hyperventilating (feeling dizzy, tingling in fingers or toes), hold a paper bag over your mouth and nose and breathe in and out until the tingling goes away. (It will.)

19. If you decide to bail out, okay. See if you can hold on for two more minutes before you do.

20. Remember: Your mind and body are running a big bluff – that something terrible is happening. It isn't. You've been here before. Thousands of people have been here many thousands of times before. It's okay. It feels awful. It's still okay

21. Write down what is so awful about it. Your heart beating fast? Feeling faint? Being scared of what these things might mean? If you could get rid of just one of your sensations, which one would you choose? Write it down. Also, write down why you chose that one.

22. Time it. Before bailing out, see if you can remain in your panic attack longer than last time.

23. Do not forget to be writing down the time and severity of each symptom every 5 minutes. You will want to know how these progress when you review all this from your calm state later.

24. Do not forget your thoughts. Are you catastrophizing? Are you thinking you are a failure? Are you making assumptions about the future? Can you think of something positive about yourself? Write it down.

## Experiments

One of the healthiest ways to approach our experience is to be without preconceptions. This leaves it open for unexpected possibilities to occur.

My father demonstrated this over and over. He was endlessly sociable. He simply loved to talk with people. So he constantly started conversations with whoever crossed his path, ending up as friends with the most unlikely characters.

Once, in the middle of New York City, we had to pull over to the curb in a not-very-nice part of town and wait while someone ran into a particular store. A large and derelict guy approached the car and I went for the door locks. To my shock, my father got out of the car and started one of his involved conversations about God knows what. It was obviously rewarding to each of them since they both resisted breaking it off when it came time to leave. So much for my preconceptions.

## Experiment # 1

This experiment is to get out and do things that you are inhibited about. It is fine to have others along – especially members of your group who are doing the same experiment.

(As Piglet said when going to capture the heffalump: "It's so much friendlier with two.")

You and you friends can write out a list of things that are hard for you to do. (It became a standing joke in our treatment groups that you had better not tell Dr. E that you had trouble with something because your next assignment would be to do it.) Are you people-pleasers (by any chance)? Then confront this by thinking up little experiments involving not pleasing people. For example, it may conflict with your people-pleasing self to return items to the store. If so, you and your friend can do the experiment of buying things at 5 stores and then returning them.

As in meditation, pay attention to what happens. Does everyone sigh or give you a dirty look when you come to make your return? Do some store employees treat it as no different from making a sale? How do you feel throughout the process? Are you timid and apologetic to begin with? Do some store personnel make you feel better about yourself? If so, what precisely did they do that triggered that response in you? Do other store personnel make you feel bad? What was the difference? Did some act as though they were doing you a big favor? Did some imply somehow that you did not deserve what you were asking for? How did they imply that? Can you put that look on your own face and say their words the way they did? Practice it with your partner until you've got it down pat. On whom can you try out that look and tone later? Are there other options for how you can feel in response? Or, do you always feel one way if they take a certain tone with you?

Also, try different things. Try abject apology for taking up their valuable time. Lay it on thick. Then, in another store, be snooty and try acting as though you completely deserve to be refunded your money. Or, try to create the impression that you completely do not deserve the refund. Somewhere else, try being friendly – like complimenting them on something they are wearing or asking how it is to work in that job. Do people respond differently depending upon how you behave? Or, are they in their own worlds and it wouldn't matter if you came in the store naked?

## Experiment # 2

Do you have trouble saying 'no'? (Need I ask?) Well, go through a whole day saying 'no' to everything anyone asks you to do. Make a note describing each time you said 'no' and what happened. You can even it up later by going through a day saying 'yes' to everything you are asked to do. And you should. Because by saying 'yes' to everything, you will learn some astonishing things about what that does – to you and to others.

## Experiment # 3

This experiment involves desensitizing to people thinking that you are weird or crazy. How do you do this? By deliberately doing things to get this response. A common assignment in the supermarket was having to buy one grape. No, you were not allowed to let them give it to you. You had to go to the Produce section and have the man weigh and price one grape. Then, you had to go through checkout and pay for it.

So you and your partner in this can think up things you can do to get people to think you are strange. (That's one of your fears, right?) Here are some examples:

- Go to the shoe store to try on shoes wearing different shoes on each foot. (Both of you.)

- Give passing strangers gratuitous positive predictions of their futures.

- Go to the ice cream parlor and have them give you a scoop into a crystal cup you brought with you. Eat it there.

- Go to the meat counter of a store and ask for cat meat. Say you heard that Chinese restaurants serve it.

- Hand out dandelion bouquets to passersby.

The reactions you get can be amazing. One of my favorite experiences from going on field trips happened with Linda – a 4'10" tall person who drove 18-wheeler trucks. (How she saw over the steering wheel, I never knew.)

A group of patients and therapists had gone to a supermarket for a field trip. It suddenly occurred to me that with Linda being so small, she could easily fit in the shopping cart. So I lifted her in and we went all through the store with me pushing the cart. She took a number and we waited through the Deli line. When the man handed our purchase over the counter, she reached for it and put it in the cart with her. We then went through the checkout line in the front of the store – Linda still in the cart, now putting our groceries on the conveyor belt. Nobody batted an eyelash. Finally, I just had to ask the checkout guy whether he did not see anything unusual in what we were doing. He responded: "Not really. You see, I'm the manager of the store and this isn't anything compared to what I've seen here!" (If you are feeling pity for Linda being put through this, don't. Afterwards, she always told people that this was the turning point that led to her cure.)

# Assignments for Chapter 14

## 1. Experiment

Make a list of 5 more experiments with the world you and your friends can try. Think of doing things you have never heard of anyone doing. You and your friends can do this together – but invent 5 per person.

## 2. Field Trips

Make dates with your friends for carrying out your experiments.

## 3. Continue your Anxiety Diary and Anxiety Chart

## 4. Systematic Desensitization

Continue working your way through that Phobic Hierarchy.

# CHAPTER FIFTEEN

## Marriage and Family

### Or

### New Experiences For Everybody

There was a researcher who found that people could not stay in a new place more than 2 months without adapting to it. They would automatically start considering it as home and would make adjustments in the place and in their thinking accordingly. (You know – put up tacky curtains, boil some cabbage, get an Elvis clock, call it "my pad" and so on.)

In the same way, people cannot live together very long without adapting to each other. Pretty soon, they form patterns of behavior in response to each other. Like if I always leave my shoes in the middle of the room, you will not trip over them many times before you begin to look out for them (or throw them out of the window).

## Getting Stuck In A Role

One of the basic principles of Family Therapy is that people who live together, develop a system of behaviors and attitudes towards each other. Roles within the family are created such as the pre-agoraphobic child often being "the strong one" as we discussed earlier. As time goes by, the roles become more and more solidified until they are just taken for granted. No one questions the truth of them and soon people become so used to them that their presence is forgotten. However, not only do their effects remain, but they also become all the stronger for not being consciously seen. They get "set in concrete" and people start feeling trapped without really knowing what is trapping them.

Here's how this can happen:

Mom has gone out with her friends for a couple of hours, leaving Dad with 5-year-old Mary Lou and baby Freddie. Freddie starts crying and Dad cannot figure out what he wants. Freddie just keeps wailing and howling. Mary Lou says: "Give him to me." She begins rocking him in her arms and singing to him. Soon Freddie has quieted down.

What happens the next time the situation is repeated? Naturally, Dad turns to Mary Lou. Wouldn't you?

Mary Lou is quite proud of her ability to take over for Mom and soothe Freddie. She feels like a big girl and she admonishes Dad that "Men just don't know how to take care of babies."

Mary Lou is easing into the role of substitute mom. She likes it, Dad likes it and obviously Freddie likes it. When Dad tells Mom about what happened, they agree that maybe Mary Lou "is good with kids." Mary Lou glows when she hears this.

As similar situations arise, Mary Lou seeks out opportunities to live up to her new role. She presses to care for Freddie even when Mom is present. When a new baby comes into the family, she is all set. She has cared for Freddie throughout the pregnancy and she happily spells mom with the baby whenever she is allowed. Mom agrees that she may as well permit this because by now everyone knows that "Mary Lou has a way with kids." (The concrete has set.)

Later on, there will be times when Mary Lou wants to just be a kid herself and will regret being trapped in the role of kid care-taker. But she and the rest of the family will have accepted the "fact" that kid care taking is just what comes naturally to Mary Lou. (Also, pretty handy for the others who would rather not do the care taking themselves.)

The moral is that together, we and others inadvertently collude in setting up roles, and later we wonder how we ever got stuck in them.

Here's where all this was going: *Having Panic Disorder is a role.* In other words, certain things are expected of you as an agoraphobic. You are expected to be dependent upon your "safe persons" (husband, kids, friends) to enable you to go various places. You are expected to rely upon others to go places for you – like shopping. The whole family may expect not to be able to take certain kinds of vacations (such as cruises) because of your Panic Disorder. You may be expected to be "the skeleton in the closet" – namely, the crazy person for whom everyone must cover up and make excuses lest the dark secret come out. And, as you are doubtless aware, you may be allowing everyone to feel good about themselves by virtue of their superiority to you – the weak one.

If you stop having panic attacks, you will have stopped playing that role. But as we have seen with Mary Lou, getting out of a role may not be so easy. It may meet with resistance from ourselves and from others who have come to count on our being a certain way. So as you make efforts to become an independent individual, you can expect this to upset the balance of roles in your home. Your husband may mysteriously begin to feel that you do not love him as much as before. (After all, you do not need him in the ways that you formerly did.) Their being superior to you will no longer be there to bolster the self-esteem of your spouse and children. People may feel threatened by your new independence of them. They may worry that you will leave them if you are no longer forced to stay by your panic attacks. Panic had created a comfortable security about you – that you were always going to be there because, after all, you could not go anywhere else. Now, you are upsetting the apple cart.

As a result, you may experience various kinds of resistance to changing your role to that of non-agoraphobic. Your spouse and children may be much more willing than usual to cater to your phobic needs – to go places with or for you. You will need to be sensitive to their possibly feeling rejected when you turn down such offers. It helps if you show appreciation for the offer and possibly suggest some other kind of help they can do for you. (Of course, if you ask the kids to clean their room, you will quickly cure them of offering.)

On the other hand, it is quite human for them to feel: "Okay, if you think you are so darned independent, let's see you take a plane to visit your mother in L.A. by yourself." You will need to patiently explain that just because you are learning to swim does not mean that you are ready for the English Channel.

Your spouse and family need to know that they can still be very helpful for you. But the kind of help you need at this point is support for your efforts to break free of the restrictions imposed by panic. This help also involves benefits for them. They get to be free of having to do all sorts of things with and for you that formerly you could not do yourself. In fact, you will have to ask them to refuse to curtail their activities as a result of some agoraphobic need you have. Because this has been "enabling" you.

## What "Enabling" Is

The concept of "enabling" comes from alcoholism treatment. It refers to the phenomenon that many of the adaptations family members make to the fact of someone's drinking inadvertently encourage it. Thus, when the alcoholic is hung over and the spouse calls work or friends for him to say that he is ill, that spouse is saving him from some of the consequences of his drinking. This <u>enables</u> him to drink without suffering that particular consequence. The more consequences his family saves him from, the more he is enabled to drink without paying the price for it. Needless to say, this is no help to him. It just delays his bottoming out. This is why support groups for family members, such as Al-Anon, insist that the best help for a drinker is for family members to not protect him from the consequences of his drinking.

Sorry, but the same goes for you: having to deal with the consequences of your Panic Disorder is the best help your family can be for you. Covering up the fact of your panics is not help, as you have seen in the Assignment for Chapter 8. Likewise, your family should not skip that trip or outing because panic prevents you from going along. You want to experience the unpleasant effects of your condition. And you need to experience them in order to have the motivation to carry out some of the more difficult assignments. Also, you will feel a sense of freedom if you do not always have to feel that you are an inconvenience to other people. They are free to go if they wish and you are free not to. You don't owe anybody.

So, your family gets to be free of some of the restrictions imposed upon them by your Panic Disorder. This is something positive that they get out of the role shift and changed relationship with you. In other words, they may be losing your dependence upon them, but they are gaining in being less restricted by your condition.

Another role change you will need to make is to stop being a doormat. Instead, you will need to assert yourself.

## Assertiveness

A few years ago assertiveness and Assertiveness Training were all the rage. People were told to do some pretty obnoxious things in the name of assertiveness. Like blankly repeating some request over and over until you got your way. (There is a term in Psychiatry for this kind of behavior - and it is not looked upon as a compliment.)

On the other hand, we have already noted that "doormatism" is a common problem amongst agoraphobics. So, if you are not to insist upon your own way and you are also looking to not be walked upon, what can you do? The answer is what I consider to be true assertiveness, as opposed to aggressiveness. True assertiveness consists of recognizing your position and stating it while neither giving in to the other person nor insisting upon getting your way.

How is this done? Pretty simple (but – you guessed it – not always easy). You express yourself in statements such as: "I feel shut out when you watch TV from dinner until bedtime." Please note: this statement does not tell the other person: "You shouldn't watch TV from dinner until bedtime." It does not make threats or lay blame such as: "You must have problems with intimacy if you watch TV from dinner until bedtime." Or: "If you are going to ignore me after dinner, do not expect me to want to make love when we go to bed." What your statement does do is to state how you feel. Period. If the other person wants to do something about how you feel, he is free to ask what you have in mind. If not, you will be left to deal with your feelings yourself. And you can do so in whatever way is true to yourself. This may mean going to the movies with a friend. Or by going to bed early (for yourself, not to punish).

Another example: "I feel taken for granted when I work for an hour making dinner and you do not show any appreciation of it." Again, you are just stating the facts. You are not blaming your feelings on the other person. Nor are you blaming yourself for having them. You are simply being true to yourself by stating how you feel.

Statements such as these do not set up an argument. How can someone argue with how you feel? You feel as you do. There is no fault. It is simply the fact. If the other person wants to say that it should not be the fact and that it's your own fault, they are entitled to their opinion. Right or wrong, it is still the fact. If they hurt your feelings in responding to your telling them the fact, you can (and should) tell them that. If they keep on hurting your feelings and you do not want to stay around for more of it, you should state that and leave if they do not respond in a way that does not hurt.

For example:

You: "I feel taken for granted when I work at making dinner for an hour and you do not show any appreciation of it."

Spouse: "Well, you are too sensitive. You should learn to get along without my having to constantly compliment you."

You: "It hurts my feelings for you to say there's something wrong with me for feeling the way I do. How I feel is how I feel."

Spouse: "Too bad. How I feel is that you should get a life. Then you wouldn't need me to be complimenting you all the time."

You: "I just feel more put down when you say that."

Spouse: "You always feel put down. It's your favorite place to be – the put down victim."

You: "If we can't come up with anything better than your telling me everything that's wrong with me, then I don't want to stay in this conversation any more."

Spouse: "What do you <u>want</u> us to come up with?

You: "That you love me and that it matters to you if my feelings get hurt. And that it's not wrong of me to want some acknowledgement from you that I really worked at making us dinner."

Spouse: "Well, of course I love you. And I do appreciate your making dinner."

You: "Well, I love you, too. I guess that's why it's so easy to feel hurt if it doesn't feel completely mutual."

Spouse: "Well, it is. It really is."

This, of course, is one of the more difficult ways the discussion could have gone – that all you were getting from your spouse was various criticisms, so you had to offer him the choice of either treating you differently or you would not stay in the conversation. Indeed, the only worse way would be for the communication to have broken down completely. I have chosen this example on purpose to show how you can stick to your guns of being true to yourself while not blaming either yourself or the other person. In many, if not most, situations, you will find that your unblaming statement of "I feel…" will be responded to with caring about how you feel.

It is important to practice making such unblaming statements – both in and outside of the situation. If you got hurt and did not say anything, you can think later about what you should have said. If the hurt does not go away, go ahead and say what you should have said. Remember – the goal is being true to yourself. It does not depend upon what the other person responds.

I would suggest that you ask your spouse to read this chapter. It will explain what you will be doing differently and your spouse's role in your treatment. It will also be extremely useful for good communication between you if your spouse practices making assertive statements on his own behalf, as well. After all, the only winning is when both of you win.

# Assignments for Chapter 15

## 1. Roles

Identify each person's role in your family.

## 2. Involve Your Family

Ask your family to read this chapter. Ask them to identify each person's role. Compare your lists.

## 3. Enabling

Ask everyone not to enable you anymore.

## 4. Assertiveness

Start practicing making assertive, unblaming "I feel…" statements.

## 5. Ongoing Exercises

Continue your Anxiety Diary, Anxiety Chart, Field Trips and Systematic Desensitization.

# CHAPTER SIXTEEN

## The Goal Of Treatment

### Or

### "A fear is like a cowardly dog: If you run from it, it will chase you. If you turn and look it in the eye, it will back down."
### Mok Tzu

At first glance, it would seem that the goal of treatment is obvious – not having any more panic attacks. But there are problems with making this your goal.

First, how would you know that you had ever reached it? If you did not have a panic attack for six months, you still would not know whether you would have one the next day.

Second, if you <u>did</u> have one the next day, would you conclude that your goal had not been reached? What if you did not have one for one year? Or two? Eventually, it would be pretty silly to say that having one panic attack in that length of time meant you were not over your Panic Disorder.

Third, never having another panic attack is just, plain unrealistic. If that were the requirement for a medication to be considered effective, no medication would ever be approved for just about anything. One study showed that antibiotics – which are one of the most effective medications – work about 70% of the time. As previously discussed, a medication is approved for a given use if it can be shown to have a statistically better result than a placebo ("sugar pill"). This means that drugs are routinely approved which either had no effect or only a partial effect in many of the people who took them.

So, if our definition of cure was to never have another panic attack, we would certainly have a standard that was far higher than medications are required to achieve. (In fairness to the medication proponents, I want you to know that in some studies of medication effects, some of the subjects did become panic-free for the length of the study.)

Lastly, what if you were to have a truly "spontaneous" panic attack? You know – one that truly "came out of the blue" - a panic attack that had no discernable reason? Maybe one that just happened because of a combination of the barometric pressure, your agoraphobic physiology, some fluorescent lights and the full moon? Or, that famous chemical imbalance? Would that mean that you were never cured – that you had never "gotten over" your Panic Disorder?

Obviously, the answer is 'No'. If a person had learned and applied all that is in this book, changed her life, learned the meaning of her panic attacks, gotten out of her Life Traps and Day-to-Day Traps, overcome the "habit" of panic reactions to various situations and straightened out her Cognitive Mistakes, surely the existence of one or two spontaneous panic attacks every year would not mean that she was not cured. (And between zero and two per year is typically what is left for a person who completes this program.)

## So What **Is** Being "Cured"?

Well, what if there was something that was far better than going through life hoping you would not have another panic attack? There is, you know. It is being able to go about your life knowing for a fact that if you did have another panic attack, you could handle it. Knowing you'd be fine. Knowing that a panic attack would not make you doubt yourself and all you had learned in the course of overcoming panic. Knowing that a panic attack could not control your future actions, make you limit where you went or with whom. And knowing that panic attack or no panic attack, you were free to do as you choose!

That is what I call cured.

And if you compare this result with counting on some medication to keep you from having panic attacks – and worrying that they will return if you stop the pills – then I think you will agree that this is a vastly better outcome.

*So, in the end, it is necessary to desensitize yourself to the panic attacks themselves!*

You can only do this by having them and learning to be comfortable with them. Not enjoy them. Who likes to feel her heart pounding, rubbery knees and so on? Although, if they were occurring because you were in love, you would not be complaining. So, it's a matter of what those sensations mean to you. You can learn that those sensations do not mean anything special. They can simply mean: "Oh, it's one of those darn panic attacks again." Really. Lots of people have done it.

You can learn to regard them in just the same way that people feel about all sorts of physical and mental conditions that occur occasionally and which do not mean much of anything except that they have to be put up with while they are there. There are conditions of intermittent weakness, conditions of trick knees, backs that go out, sugar or electrolytes that get out of balance, hard-to-stabilize seizures, cluster headaches, painful and crippling arthritis, manic episodes, narcolepsy, heart arrhythmias, disabling PMS, recurrent depression and so on. No one likes having them, but they only need to interfere with your life as much as they actually do – not more because of your reaction to them.

Remember my early patient who was disrupting his whole life because of his attitude about what went on with him for 40 minutes a week? His reaction to the problem was much more disabling than the problem itself.

So, the final step in your cure of Panic Disorder is to learn not to react to having to sit out a panic attack. And when you have done this, they almost never occur. After all, without the reaction, there is no Catastrophic Thinking or Anticipatory Anxiety to bring on a panic attack.

## Assignment for Chapter 16

The assignment, then, is to go out into the world, seeking to have a panic attack!! No kidding!! (This actually may not be so easy to do since there is often a so-called "paradoxical effect" – namely, that when you look for it, it does not happen. But this is useful learning, too.) Of course, if you have a panic attack without seeking one, that is also fine. Or, you can go to places or situations where you are very likely to have a panic attack (with a helpful person standing by, if you like).

Before doing this, you and your friend can carry out a number of "dry runs" in your home. You can also do imaginal work as in Chapter Nine by going through having panic attacks in your imagination. Do this by practicing in your mind what you are going to feel and what you are going to do when you go have the real thing. Make your imagined experience as realistic as you can. Repeat this until you are really comfortable with going out into the world to have a panic attack.

Then, when you do go out, study your panic attack using the "Reminders and Instructions In Case of A Panic Attack." Your friend or partner can help by reading you the questions and noting down your answers. She can also help you keep on task – studying the panic attack – rather than running around in circles, pulling fire alarms or destructively tearing up this book. If you feel that you absolutely **must** leave and stop the panic attack, that is okay. But don't let that place become part of an avoidance pattern. Either return the next day and finish having your panic attack there or systematically desensitize yourself to that place. Remember: *A fear not faced will become the center of your life*. When you feel ready, give yourself experiences of having panic attacks without a "safe person" there.

Keep studying everything about your panic attacks until there is no mystery - until you know every little reaction of your body and mind that goes into having one. And repeat this until you can truly feel that: "Oh, there that is again. I will have to take time out to put up with it before I can continue about my business." *And nothing more!*

When you have completed this assignment, you can reward yourself as lavishly as you like. You can go for broke because, as I am sure you realize, *it's all over!* <u>All</u> over!! You have graduated.

## After word

The real reward is in all the growing as a person you have accomplished. You have developed skills and had experiences that will support you and help others for the rest of your life. You will discover that you have learned much more than you realize. You are now a member of an elite group of people: People who did not take the easy way out. People who were seeking, instead, to learn from what was going wrong in their lives. People whose problems became the opportunity to grow into doing life better. People who suffered and struggled and overcame much in themselves that would hold them back from fully living the life they were given. People who earned their freedom by wrestling with the angel until it blessed them.

Congratulations! You have grown wings. Enjoy flying.

# About Face

## Or

## Why This Book?

I first encountered Panic Disorder in 1971 during the first year of my residency training in Psychiatry. Nobody knew much about it at the time. My patients and I struggled our way through it – doing pretty well, in retrospect. About 8 years later, I was asked to join with some other therapists to create a treatment program for Agoraphobics. We used everything we knew or could find out to help our patients. With one exception: we did not use medications other than a few Valium pills for our patients to carry with them for emergencies. There were two reasons for this. First, we believed that psychological problems were an invitation to grow; and second, for those who just wanted a pill to make their symptoms go away, a clinic was there, in Boston, providing just that.

Like most experimental programs, ours was young, enthusiastic, open to all ideas, ready to drop what did not work and very interested in what the patients had to say. It was incredibly successful. When we were on local TV talk shows, they were flooded with callers. Needless to say, we had no difficulty getting patients.

In those days, psychiatrists were often trained to do an extensive evaluation of prospective patients before starting treatment. This evaluation included an exhaustive review of the patient's entire biography: where they were at each point in their lives, who were they with, what they did and, especially, why they made each choice in their lives as they did. You were not finished until you "knew what made the person tick."

When designing our program, the therapists and I decided that we should begin with such an evaluation to be done by me. This meant that I ended up knowing, in great detail, the entire life stories of every patient we treated. My residency had taught me a very valuable skill: not what were the causes of every kind of problem that came my way, but how to discover those causes. When this was put together with the biographies of all our patients, it was pretty inevitable that the common denominator in all those life stories would emerge. And it did. They were all trapped!

Using this understanding, the therapists continued working together and refining the treatment for several years. The program became well-established. Many, many patients went through the program and found their freedom from Panic and Agoraphobia. And naturally, the newness wore off.

Eventually, some of us developed interests in other directions and made plans to leave the program and the area to pursue these. Many of our former patients let out a very gratifying howl of indignation: "How could you even consider stopping your work with Agoraphobia?" "You've got something here no one else has an inkling of." "You just <u>can't</u> quit now that you've figured it out." "You should at least write it down." And so forth.

We hugged them (you were allowed to in those days) and told them that we were not unique. Others were increasingly working with Panic and would doubtless discover what we had. We explained that for our own growth, it was time to move on. Reluctantly, we said our farewells.

Over the years since then, I have worked with many therapists, attended many lectures and read many journal articles always expecting to find what we had discovered back then. I'm still sure it's out there, but every time I explain our understanding of Panic and Agoraphobia to other therapists or to new patients, they respond as if someone has opened the curtains and let in the light. In fact, I recently listened to a lecture for Psychiatrists by an eminent authority in which he said that Agoraphobia was really the fear of death!! (Can you imagine?!) So the time has come to write it all down for anyone who wants to use it. Then, the next time a patient or therapist asks what is going on in Panic and Agoraphobia, I will be able to say: "Read this. Here it all is, as much as I know."

There is nothing about my understanding of the causes and cures of these problems that is beyond the average person. It therefore made the best sense to me to write this for panic sufferers to use themselves. One of the original therapists had been an agoraphobic who had worked her own way out of it before almost anything was known. Using the excellent treatment methods that have been developed since then, you should have little trouble learning what to do to overcome Panic and Agoraphobia. Your struggle is with getting yourself to do it and thereby overcome your fears. For support, encouragement and other peoples' ideas, I have suggested that you work this program with others who have this problem, either in or outside a group. And for your safety, I have suggested that you work under the supervision of a trained professional.

Some words about this manual:

It is organized with informational chapters followed by assignments as much as possible relating to the information just presented. Since many of the assignments out in the field would not make much sense without a lot of the information, the manual is more educational towards the beginning and involves more of going out and having experiences towards the end. Thus, you can go through the early chapters fairly rapidly and you will probably need to spend more time from Chapter 9 on. One possible schedule is to spend one week on each of Chapters 1 through 8 and then 2 weeks on each of the following chapters. Depending upon how intensively you go about your field work, you may have completed all of it in this amount of time or less. Or, you may wish to take it more gradually. Remember: the total amount of time you spend doing your field work is what counts – not how quickly or slowly you put in your time. The original treatment evolved into a 15-week program - so that gives you an idea of how quickly you can successfully carry out this program if you want.

I have attempted to make the writing as light as possible for all our sakes. This reflects the fact that in the original program, there was much laughter along with the tears, white knuckles, showdowns and all the rest. Although the growth you achieve through working this treatment program may be one of the most important steps you ever take, there is no reason not to have fun doing it where you can. When we can laugh at ourselves, things go so much more easily.

## An overview of the program:

In case you're interested in a summary of what's in this manual, here it is: Chapters 1 through 3 are highly informational although their assignments get you going on overcoming your Panic and Agoraphobia. Chapter 1 gives you the definitions of Agoraphobia and the Panic Disorders. Chapter 2 tells you what goes on in your body when you are experiencing the symptoms of Panic. Chapter 3 gives you information about how an agoraphobic's body is different from the bodies of non-agoraphobics. The understanding of Panic and Agoraphobia to which I have been referring is what you find in Chapter 4 – The Key To Panic Disorder. Just as Chapters 2 and 3 tell you how your body works, Chapters 5 and 6 describe how your mind works. (While you are learning these things about how you function, in the assignments, you are beginning the process of change.) Chapter 7 gives you an overview of the main kinds of treatment that exist for Panic and Agoraphobia. In it is advice for choosing a therapist if you decide to go that route. You learn about the major medications being used nowadays in Chapter 8. In Chapters 9 through 12, you learn principles and techniques from the major forms of therapy and how to put them to use yourself. Chapter 13 teaches you meditation – probably the most widely growing technique for relaxation and insight in this country today. In Chapter 14, you get some of the hardest and most whimsical work to change your view of the world around you and your relationship with it. Bringing your marriage and family into the picture of you as a non-agoraphobic is the subject of Chapter 15. And finally, Chapter 16 contains the discovery of what "cure" really means. It gives you the final step to take in overcoming Panic.

As you can see, I have found that the program in this manual works. Some of it is mainstream Psychiatry and some is not. Where I depart the most from the treatment that is increasingly being offered by Psychiatrists nowadays is with regard to medication. There is a growing acceptance in Psychiatry of the idea that mental disorders are biologically caused and that they should be treated with medications. I don't agree. I believe that many of the milder disorders, including Panic Disorder, have psychological reasons behind them. These reasons can be understood. By understanding them and taking psychological steps, people can grow. This not only results in overcoming the condition, but people also attain better, healthier and more fulfilling lives. And I have seen it happen over and over again. So that is the approach in this program – mainstream or not.

Finally, as I said in the Preface, this book is for your liberation. It points you to where many others have found freedom. You have all the resources you need to walk this path. Just keep putting one foot in front of the other and your success is inevitable.

Mark Eisenstadt, M.D.
Agoraphobia-Treatment.com
January, 2012

# RECOMMENDED READING

Cheri Huber "There Is Nothing Wrong With You", "The Fear Book" and many others. Keep It Simple Books, 1993.

Claire Weekes "Hope And Help For Your Nerves" and "Peace From Nervous Suffering." Signet Books, 1993 and 1991.

## About Cognitive Therapy:

David Burns, M.D. "Feeling Good" and "The Feeling Good Workbook." Wm. Morrow and Co., 1980.

## About Meditation:

Joseph Goldstein "The Experience Of Insight" Shambala Publications, Inc., 1976.

Stephen Levine "A Gradual Awakening" Anchor Books, 1979.

# REFERENCES

Alcoholics Anonymous World Services, Inc. "Twelve Steps And Twelve Traditions", 1996.

Al-anon Group Family Head, Inc. "One Day At A Time In Al-Anon" AFG, 1988.

"Diagnostic And Statistical Manual of Mental Disorders DSM-IV-TR (Text Revision)" American Psychiatric Press, 4th Edition, 2000.

Barbara Gordon "I'm Dancing As Fast As I Can" Bantam Books; Reissue Edition, 1987.

Joel S. Goldsmith "Man Was Not Born To Cry" Acropolis Books, Inc., 1998.

Manuel Zane. M.D. "I Never Stayed In The Dark Long Enough." Audiotape available from The Anxiety and Phobia Treatment Center, White Plains Hospital Center, (914) 681-1038.

www.ingramcontent.com/pod-product-compliance
Lightning Source LLC
Chambersburg PA
CBHW031149270326
41931CB00006B/206